The ESSE[barcode: D0103789] of

CANADIAN HISTORY

Canada since 1867:
The Post-Confederate Nation

Rae Murphy, Ph.D.
Professor, Department of History
Conestoga College
Kitchener, Ontario

Research and Education Association
61 Ethel Road West
Piscataway, New Jersey 08854

THE ESSENTIALS®
OF CANADIAN HISTORY
Canada since 1867:
The Post-Confederate Nation

Printed in the United States of America

Library of Congress Catalog Card Number 93-85678

International Standard Book Number 0-87891-917-1

ESSENTIALS is a registered trademark of
Research and Education Association, Piscataway, New Jersey 08854

What the "Essentials of History" Will Do for You

REA's "Essentials of History" series offers a new approach to the study of history that is different from what has been available previously. Each book in the series has been designed to steer a sensible middle course, by including neither too much nor too little information.

Compared with conventional history outlines, the "Essentials of History" offer far more detail, with fuller explanations and interpretations of historical events and developments. Compared with voluminous historical tomes and textbooks, the "Essentials of History" offer a far more concise, less ponderous overview of each of the periods they cover.

The "Essentials of History" are intended primarily to aid students in studying history, doing homework, writing papers and preparing for exams. The books are organized to provide quick access to information and explanations of the important events, dates, and persons of the period. The books can be used in conjunction with any text. They will save hours of study and preparation time while providing a firm grasp and insightful understanding of the subject matter.

Instructors too will find the "Essentials of History" useful. The books can assist in reviewing or modifying course outlines. They also can assist with preparation of exams, as well as serve as an efficient memory refresher.

In sum, the "Essentials of History" will prove to be handy reference sources at all times.

The authors of the series are respected experts in their fields. They present clear, well-reasoned explanations and interpretations of the complex political, social, cultural, economic, and philosophical issues and developments which characterize each era.

In preparing these books, REA has made every effort to assure their accuracy and maximum usefulness. We are confident that each book will prove enjoyable and valuable to its user.

CONTENTS

CHAPTER 1

From British North America to Canada

1.1 Formation

The 36 colonial politicians who met in Charlottetown, Quebec, and finally in London to create the confederation of the four remaining British North American colonies, did so with varying degrees of enthusiasm. Known as the Fathers of Confederation, these politicians saw themselves first and foremost as British subjects, and they saw the nation they were to forge as an integral part of that empire and the embodiment of that heritage on the North American continent.

1.1.1 British North America Act (1867)

Until 1982, the British North America Act (B.N.A.) was the basic statute of Canada. It was described at its inception as "similar in principle to that of the United Kingdom." British monarchical and parliamentary systems were to be preserved. The B.N.A. Act was legislation of the British Parliament, and could only be amended by an act of that parliament. In its original form, the act did not grant complete political independence to Canada. Canada could not have any direct or independent dealings with other states. Its armed forces were under the command of British officers serving the monarch through the appointed Governor-General. Even the powers of internal self-government granted the Canadian Parliament under the act could be disallowed by the British Parliament.

1.1.2 July 1, 1867: The Dominion of Canada

At its constitutional birth, Canada consisted of four provinces, Ontario (formerly Canada West), Quebec (formerly Canada East), New Brunswick, and Nova Scotia. Newfoundland was originally part of the confederation discussions but did not join until 1949. Prince Edward Island, also an original participant, could not be persuaded to join until 1873. Queen Victoria chose the bustling lumber town of Bytown—renamed Ottawa—as the country's capital. Its main virtue was it was neither Montreal nor Toronto.

The structure of government reflected the British system, with a head of government (the Prime Minister), a two chamber legislature, and the monarch represented by a Governor-General. The Upper House, or Senate, corresponded to the old legislative council. Membership was based upon provincial allocations, and members were appointed—at that time—for life. The Lower House or House of Commons, corresponded to the previous legislative assembly. Its members were to be elected in numbers based roughly on provincial population (for a maximum term of five years).

Factors other than British influence were reflected in the structure of the federal government. While the House of Commons was elected in proportion to provincial populations, Quebec was seen to represent the minority French population and was guaranteed a permanent proportion of the total membership of the House regardless of future population shifts.

The recently concluded American Civil War was also a factor in the division of powers between the provinces and the federal government. Matters of national interest were legislated by the federal government and local matters—clearly and carefully enumerated—by provincial governments. All residual powers were to fall to the federal government. It was thus hoped that issues of provincial or states' rights would not arise.

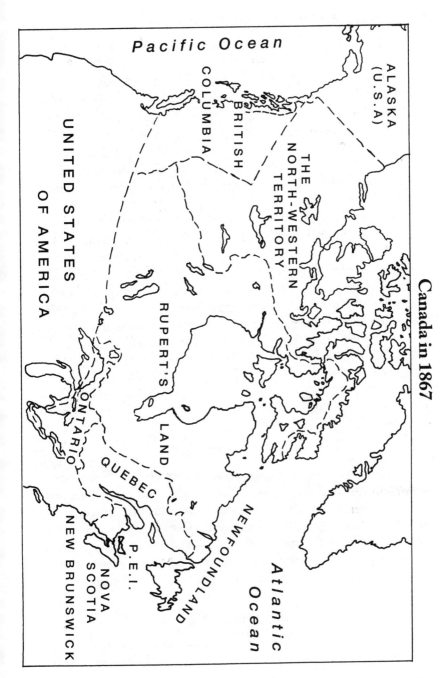

Canada in 1867

Pacific Ocean

ALASKA
(U.S.A)

BRITISH COLUMBIA

THE NORTH-WESTERN TERRITORY

UNITED STATES OF AMERICA

RUPERT'S LAND

ONTARIO

QUEBEC

NEWFOUNDLAND

P.E.I.

NOVA SCOTIA

NEW BRUNSWICK

Atlantic Ocean

1.2   1867-1873: Sir John A. Macdonald

John A. Macdonald was the obvious choice to be first Prime Minister of the Dominion. At the request of the Governor-General, he began to assemble his first cabinet before the July 1, 1867 proclamation. Macdonald quickly demonstrated his abilities in a finely balanced coalition that reflected the delicate political, regional, and religious divisions of the reluctant country. The first elections brought some surprises, in the defeat of George Brown in Ontario and all but one of the pro-confederation members from Nova Scotia. However the Conservative partnership of Macdonald and George E. Cartier remained intact and the government survived.

The government's first issue was to convince reluctant Nova Scotia to remain in Confederation. The Anti-Confederation forces had vainly tried to convince the British authorities to exclude Nova Scotia from the 1867 union. After their successes in both the federal and provincial elections of 1867, they were unsuccessful in efforts to convince Britain to repeal the B.N.A. Act. The province had also engaged in negotiations—ultimately fruitless—on an independent commercial treaty with the U.S. By 1869, Macdonald had convinced Joseph Howe, the leader of the provincial government and leader of the repeal movement, to accept a federal cabinet post for himself and a better financial arrangement for the province (including a larger grant). The repeal movement gradually diminished.

1.3   The Hudson's Bay Company

The Hudson's Bay Company owned vast tracts of land separating Canada from the Pacific coast. In 1869, an agreement was reached between the Company and the Canadian government to purchase this land. The settlement transferred the land to Canada and included a cash payment of $1500000 and 45000 acres of land around the company's existing forts. The agreement made no provision for the population of the area—mostly Métis (of mixed French and Native descent).

1.4   The First Riel Rebellion

Aside from the aboriginal population scattered about the vast territory, there was one main settlement, the Red River colony, in the south east. Neither the Natives nor the Métis—who spoke French and were Catholic—were consulted about the territory's future. The Métis were not anxious to join Canada. They captured Fort Gary (now Winnipeg) and formed a "provisional government" led by Louis Riel. A few Protestant Canadians who lived in the territory refused to accept the authority of the provisional government. One, Thomas Scott, was executed by the government. This caused an uproar in Ontario, and John A. Macdonald was under tremendous pressure to put the rebellion down by force. However, opinion in Quebec was sympathetic towards Riel.

Macdonald finally chose to negotiate, and an agreement was reached whereby the Red River colony became the province of Manitoba. The Manitoba Act of 1870 spelled out the conditions under which the land titles of the colony would be respected; and in the uninhabited part of the land, the federal authorities would oversee railway construction and settlement.

Many reasons have been given for Macdonald's compromise. Aside from the internal political and religious divisions which were sparked by the rebellion, the main issue was the "race" with the United States to occupy and control the West. The Alaska purchase, and the discovery of gold in the Yukon, brought thousands of Americans north. With the American west beginning to fill, the prairies were seen by many would-be-settlers as the "last best West." The remaining independent British Colony in North America, British Columbia, was considering joining Canada. But it was also under some pressure to join the American union. Thus, there was every reason to bring the Manitoba issue to a speedy conclusion.

While agreeing to the Manitoba compromise, Macdonald also sent troops to the territory to arrest Riel. The British supported Macdonald and also sent some British troops. This show of strength was meant to impress the Americans with Canada's determination to establish rule in the former Hudson Bay territories. Riel himself escaped arrest by fleeing to the United States.

1.5   1873: British Columbia in Confederation

Deeply in debt at the end of the gold rush, spokesmen for British Columbia promoted Confederation as a solution to the colony's financial problems.

There was actually another issue involved—the creation of responsible government, which would be hastened by joining Canada. Negotiations finally began in Ottawa. Ottawa quickly agreed to assume the colony's debt and to subsidize future public works. It also agreed to facilitate responsible government once the colony became a province. The most ambitious and controversial promise Ottawa made was to begin construction, within two years, of a transcontinental railway.

British Columbia officially entered the Canadian union on July 20, 1871.

1.6   Prince Edward Island

On the other side of Canada, this small island colony faced bankruptcy trying to complete a provincial railway. Macdonald promised a bailout and agreed to finance its completion. The federal government also agreed to a permanent financial subsidy and to provide a link to to the mainland. These promises convinced Prince Edward Island to join Confederation in 1873. Thus, by 1873, six years after confederation, Canada became a transcontinental nation—from sea to sea.

1.7   The Treaty of Washington 1871

This treaty was basically a set of Anglo-American agreements to untangle relationships between the two countries following the American Civil War. Macdonald was invited to participate—not as Prime Minister of Canada, but as one member of the five member British delegation—because much of the fallout from the negotiations would affect Canada. Canada also had some issues it wanted settled with the United States. There was a dispute over east coast fisheries; Canada wanted to restore a reciprocity agreement abrogated by the Americans. In the end, Macdonald was instructed to sign a treaty which gave Americans free access to the Atlantic fishery, and which did not include any provision for trade reciprocity.

The treaty was seen in Canada as a humiliation. It became part of the mounting criticism of Macdonald, which included his expensive financial promises to the provinces, the cost overruns on the Intercolonial Railway, and the extravagant promise of the Continental Railway to the Pacific.

1.8   The Federal Election of 1872

The first election since Confederation saw Macdonald in some difficulties. Canada's population was stagnating at about four million people. Indeed, over the past decade more people had left the country than emigrated to it. Many Canadians had emigrated to booming post Civil War United States. The world-wide depression of the 1870's was just beginning to affect Canada, and Macdonald was being sharply criticized for his inability to secure trade reciprocity with the United States during the Washington Treaty negotiations.

Macdonald nonetheless easily withstood the criticism. He generally received credit for Canada's creation and the country's successful consolidation after Confederation. Yet the ingredients of his successful election campaign were to haunt him.

CHAPTER 2

The Liberal Interlude

2.1 The Pacific Scandal: The Transcontinental Railway

Canada's railway was always a contentious issue. Macdonald decided that construction could best be handled by private enterprise, with government participation limited to land grants to the company. Two major groups, one based in Toronto and one in Montreal, bid for the project. When it proved impossible for both groups to join efforts, Macdonald seemed to favor the Montreal group headed by financier Sir Hugh Allan. Allan was forced to purge his group of American support before being awarded the contract. Allan himself had given large donations to Macdonald's Conservative Party for the extravagant election campaign of 1872. When the Opposition discovered the donations (information that was given by the disgruntled American investors cut out of the bid), the so-called Pacific Scandal erupted. It forced Macdonald's resignation. In the election that followed the Liberal Party under Alexander Mackenzie assumed power.

2.2 Alexander Mackenzie

The new prime minister was a Scottish immigrant stonemason, considered by most observers at the time as an efficient administrator but a poor and unimaginative leader. His term in office coincided with a world-wide economic depression. Canada, as has often been the case, was "at the mercy" of forces over which it had little control. None of the measures the government took to ease the burden of the depression seemed to work. These included a failed attempt to win a new reciprocity treaty with the United States, as well as the successful completion of the Intercolonial Railway.

Mackenzie was also burdened by the fact that the Liberal Party lacked a strong national base. Its support was almost totally within Protestant Ontario. Its Quebec wing, the Parti Rouge, was small and under fierce attack by the Catholic clergy, who drew no distinction between the Liberal Party and European liberalism (which had been condemned by the Pope in 1864). Such clerical pressure—and the reaction to it—would influence significantly the future course of Canadian politics. For the present, it narrowed the base of support for the Liberal Party. It became virtually impossible for the Liberals to govern.

2.3   Secret Ballot and Other Electoral Reform

The Liberal government initiated several important reforms, including the secret ballot and control over election expenses. The Corrupt Practices Act was passed, making bribery of civil servants a serious offense.

The Canadian Supreme Court was established, and the powers of the Governor-General were restricted. Both these acts furthered Canadian independence.

The Intercolonial Railway linking Quebec to the Maritimes—and creating an all Canadian route to the Atlantic—was completed in 1876. However, rising costs and the government's economy drive curtailed construction of the transcontinental railway. The Liberals tried to abandon the previous government's promises to British Columbia and a serious secessionist sentiment developed there.

2.4   Reciprocity

The issue of protectionist tariffs versus free trade has always been an issue in Canada, particularly in relations with the United States. In most instances, Canada split between the provinces—Ontario and Quebec—containing the bulk of Canada's infant manufacturing industries, who supported protection, versus the Maritimes, who supported free trade.

A system of trade reciprocity had existed between the United States and the British colonies since 1854, until it was abrogated by the Americans after the Civil War in 1866. Both John A. Macdonald and Alexander Mackenzie had tried to revive reciprocity but had failed.

The Liberal government responded to such rejection by raising tariffs, in the hope that domestic production would increase. But the depression only deepened, and by 1876 the opposition Conservatives demanded a thorough policy of protection. They blamed the Liberals for the economic crisis. Canada was losing population, the West remained empty, and the railway was still not finished.

The public had by now forgotten the scandals that had brought down the former Conservative government, and were no longer interested in the earnest Liberal slogan of "Honesty and Integrity."

2.5   The National Policy

In opposition, Macdonald formulated a new economic policy designed to build an industrial economy on the basis of an expanding internal market. They gave the policy the appealing title of The National Policy.

In the broadest sense, the policy was based upon a combination of higher tariffs and an energetic immigration policy—to populate the West and develop its great agricultural potential. Mass immigration and agricultural development could only succeed if the transcontinental railway was completed rapidly. The latter promise was at the core of the National Policy.

2.6   The Federal Election of 1878

The Conservatives—still led by Macdonald—were confident of victory over the Liberals, who warned the electorate to beware of the "demon protection." However the people's massive endorsement of the National Policy—via a huge 68 seat majority—surprised even the Conservatives. Alexander Mackenzie, the Liberal leader, was to retire shortly from politics. A revitalized Sir John A. Macdonald became Prime Minister again.

CHAPTER 3

Alienation and Rebellion

3.1   Building the Railway

The completion of the Intercontinental Railway was a key element of the National Policy. Macdonald moved quickly to award construction to a Montreal syndicate, controlled by George Stephen of the Bank of Montreal and Donald Smith of the Hudson's Bay Company. The Canadian Pacific Railway (CPR) was thus created as a private company but with massive government financial assistance—$25 million in cash and 25 million acres of land adjacent to the tracks. Tax exemptions were also given, and the company was assured of no competition to the south of its line for 20 years.

The CPR promised to have the line completed by 1891. During construction, the company was constantly faced with financial crises. It went back to the government for more money in 1883 and 1885. Nevertheless, the line was completed in 1885—six years ahead of schedule.

In 1885, the government could claim that the line was worth the price as it was able to transport troops quickly to put down the Riel Rebellion.

In 1886, the first transcontinental train arrived on the Pacific coast.

3.1.1   Western Agriculture: The High Cost of Farming

The creation of a viable agriculture economy in the Canadian West was also crucial to the National Policy. While this was impossible without a railway, the freight rates charged by the CPR raised the costs borne by settlers. Also, the high tariff associated with the National Policy raised costs and restricted the market. There was talk of rebellion among the settlers, and the Manitoba Farm Union was organized with a program of direct action.

3.1.2 The Return of Louis Riel

A far more serious situation threatened the aboriginal and Métis population. The goal of the government was to clear the western plains for agriculture. This meant the removal of the Métis and Indian population and the destruction of their way of life (as symbolized by the buffalo).

The Manitoba Act of 1870 was effectively undermined; and the land titles guaranteed to the Métis, as well as the treaties negotiated previously with the Indians, became meaningless. Driven from the Red River, the Métis moved to the North West Territory, only to be followed by the railway and the settlers breaking the ground for agriculture.

The aboriginal population fared even worse. Decimated by disease—nearly half the aboriginal population in what is now Alberta and Saskatchewan died of smallpox in the 1870s—and facing starvation resulting from systematic destruction of the buffalo, the people were herded onto reservations.

Instead of the promised amnesty after the rebellion of 1870, Louis Riel spent the next 15 years, as one historian said, "living as a hunted villain and a haunted visionary." Although elected three times to Parliament, he was three times refused his seat. When contacted by a Métis delegation and asked to return, he was married, living as an American citizen in Montana.

Upon arriving in Canada, Riel drew up a petition demanding redress of Métis, Indian, and white settlers' grievances. The petition was ignored, and the Métis and Indians declared independence. Riel was declared provisional president on March 19, 1895.

Within days, skirmishes occurred between the Métis and the North-West Mounted Police. Several Indian bands also rose in rebellion, and Macdonald ordered the Canadian militia west.

Several thousand soldiers arrived within weeks. Most came by train. The Métis and Indian fighters were defeated at the Battle of Batoche. Riel surrendered shortly after the battle, and the last Indian resistance crumbled in late May. The rebellion cost 200 lives and $6 million.

It represented the last resistance to settlement of the Canadian West.

3.1.3   The Trial and Execution of Louis Riel

Riel was charged with treason and tried. Although found guilty, the jury recommended mercy. But, under instructions from Ottawa, the magistrate sentenced Riel to hang.

The trial and sentence caused a storm of protest and sparked a controversy which reverberates to this day. Macdonald refused to commute the sentence and Riel was hanged in Regina on November 16, 1885.

In Quebec, Riel was seen as a martyr to the cause of French and Catholic rights. His death was seen as an example of the unequal and precarious existence of the French minority in Canada.

In the English-speaking, Protestant Ontario of the day, the sentence was seen as a just retribution for murder and rebellion. It is, however, questionable how much pressure Ontario public opinion had on Macdonald, or whether he was determined to see Riel hang to demonstrate his determination that the West be settled (and thereby Métis and Indian culture destroyed). Macdonald never denied later charges that he manipulated events, including the rebellion itself. The actions of the federal government throughout weakened—and eventually helped to destroy—its support nationally, and to virtually eliminate the Conservative Party in Quebec for 60 years.

The outcome was a permanent disaster for the Indians and Métis of the North West.

3.1.4   Federal Provincial Relations

Macdonald's notions of a strong federal authority often came into conflict with provincial governments. The federal government often simply disallowed provincial laws.

With the execution of Riel, federal relations with Quebec reached a low point. Honoré Mercier, a former Liberal, formed the Parti Nationale. He won the subsequent provincial election with a program calling for Quebec unity in the face of "Anglo-Saxon domination."

Other provinces held various grievances against the federal government. Manitoba challenged the CPR monopoly. The Maritime provinces blamed the National Policy for the depressed economy, and the legislature of Nova Scotia, in fact, passed a resolution to repeal membership in Confederation. However, it was Oliver Mowat, the Liberal premier of Ontario, who became known as the "father of provincial rights". Mowat began a series of legal challenges to federal authority. Soon, appeals to the Privy Council in England expanded provincial rights and jurisdiction at the federal government's expense.

In 1887, Premier Mercier was able to assemble most provincial premiers to a meeting in Quebec. Macdonald ignored the gathering, and it accomplished little. Nonetheless, this first provincial gathering was both a reminder of how fragile Canadian unity was and that even if Quebec often felt like an embattled minority opposing the federal government, it could, from time to time, find other provincial allies.

3.1.5 "The Old Man, The Old Flag, The Old Policy"

Old, tired, and considerably weakened, Macdonald fought one last election campaign. The railway was built, the National Policy still in place, and Canada still unified. Draping himself in the flag of the British Empire, Macdonald attacked Liberal proposals for reciprocity (free trade). He conducted a lonely but vigorous, and ultimately successful, re-election campaign. While he lost support in Ontario and Quebec, business fears about the removal of the external tariff overcame the losses. Macdonald's health, however, was broken, and he died within months of the election. The Conservative Party, leaderless and dispirited, drifted divided through several successors and fell from office in 1896.

3.2 The Manitoba School Crisis, and the Federal Election of 1896

The Manitoba School Crisis reflected the changing relationship between the anglophone and francophone populations as well as the determination of the Anglo-Saxon majority to control the settlement of the West.

The original Manitoba Act had recognized the property and cultural and linguistic claims of the Métis majority—who were French speaking and Catholic—as well as the majority of the pioneer settlers, also francophone and Catholic. After 1870, however, most new settlers were English-speaking Protestants from Ontario, the United States, and the British Isles. The ethnic composition had changed completely. Meanwhile, Quebec had turned inward. With a defensive nationalism, it took steps to preserve the French and Catholic school system in the province. Ontario acted to restrict French rights and argued that Manitoba and the new territories should also become English speaking. In 1890, Manitoba moved to abolish French as an official language, and virtually eliminated French education.

As the new Manitoba Schools Act made its way through the court system, the issue split the country. It especially split the Conservative Party, which now drew its support, ironically, from Catholic clergy in Quebec and from Protestant Ontario. The government could therefore not develop a compromise position. By 1892, when the Manitoba legislation had passed all its court challenges, the government was unable to act under provisions of the BNA Act to protect minority linguistic rights. A half-hearted attempt was allowed to die on a parliamentary order paper in 1896. These events formed the background for the federal election of 1896 in which the Conservative Party was clearly defeated and the Liberals emerged with their leader Wilfrid Laurier.

3.3   Wilfrid Laurier

Many historians contend that the true successor to John A. Macdonald was Wilfrid Laurier. While they had different personal styles. Their policies were almost identical: an external tariff, aggressive western settlement, as well as the preservation of Imperial ties. Laurier grasped, as had Macdonald, that the only force holding Canada together was an ability to forge compromises and, when this was impossible, to find a way of postponing the issue while getting on with other things. With time, effort, and the expenditure or political capital, Laurier was able finally to develop a compromise, and the Manitoba School Crisis was thus settled in 1897. The larger question of francophone rights in Manitoba was only ruled on by the Supreme Court in 1976.

3.4   The Years of Economic Growth

The economic depression which had begun in 1873, and which had caused so much havoc during the construction of the railway, was clearly over by the 1880s. The Laurier government moved away from its traditional free trade policies to supporting a protective tariff and accelerated growth policies. A number of developments—the discovery of gold in South Africa and the rapid urbanization of Europe—all opened markets for Canada's grains and base metals. The government pushed new railway lines, particularly into British Columbia, to exploit new mineral discoveries. New technological advances opened the Canadian Shield. Other land became invaluable as ground pulp could be made into paper. Other areas became sites for hydro-electric development. Nowhere was the economic growth more evident than in the rush to open, at last, the Canadian prairies.

3.4.1   "The Last Best West"

Laurier appointed Clifford Sifton as Minister of the Interior in his first administration. The aggressive minister promoted the prairies as good, fertile land. Would-be immigrants from the British Isles and the United States were encouraged to settle. But, it was Sifton's appeal to the "hardy peasants" of central Europe which would have the greatest impact on the Canadian prairies. New farms, 30 000 a year, opened. And the volume of grain production grew with the development of hardy and fast maturing strains, such as Marquis, and the advance of dry-soil farming techniques. In 1896, Canada produced eight million bushels of grain. By 1912, it produced 232 million bushels.

3.5   New Provinces and Old Constitutional Issues

Out of the boom of the last decade of the century, Laurier was able to fulfill his promise to create two new provinces out of the North-West Territories. In 1905, the provinces of Alberta and Saskatchewan were created. Their very organization, however, ignited the "schools question." Apparently, Laurier had secretly assured the Catholic bishops that the Confessional schools—as they had existed in the territories prior to 1875—would be reestablished in the new provinces. The new provinces assumed they would continue to develop a public school system along the lines of the Manitoba compromise—that is, English—and fundamentally secular.

As the issue became public, an outraged Clifford Sifton resigned, and the powerful minister from Nova Scotia, W.S. Fielding, threatened to follow. Laurier was forced to back-down. His retreat caused further cries of betrayal in Quebec, which again saw its role and place in Canada diminished.

Nevertheless, the two new provinces were formed. They had most of the rights of the other provinces, with the exception of federal control over land and resources in order to maintain existing homestead and investment regulations.

CHAPTER 4

From Colony To Nation

4.1   The Alaska Panhandle

The border between Russian Alaska and the British Pacific Northwest had been left vague when settled in 1825. At the time, nobody had much cared. However, by 1896 and the Klondike gold rush in the Canadian Yukon, the United States had purchased Alaska and was pressing its interpretation of the boundary. This put American territory between the Yukon and the Pacific coast. Canada disputed the U.S. claim and insisted that portions of the panhandle fell entirely within Canadian territory. All attempts at negotiation failed. Finally, an arbitration commission chaired by British Chief Justice Lord Alverstone awarded the land to the American side.

The award caused great resentment in Canada. It served to focus attention on the fact that Canada was emerging with a sense of its national interest, which could no longer be contained within the British Colonial Office. There were other foreign policy issues involving fundamental questions of Canada's place in the British Empire and the world.

4.1.1   The Boer War

In 1889, the descendants of European settlers in South Africa, the Boers, rebelled against the British Colonial administration. Canada, as a British colony, was expected to contribute soldiers in support of the British side in South Africa. The idea of going to war for the Empire in South Africa split Canada along the by now traditional political fault-line: Quebec and Ontario. Opinion in Ontario—indeed, in most of

Canada outside of Quebec—strongly favored participation in the war. In Quebec, opinion was even more strongly in favour of not participating. If anything, sentiment in Quebec tended to support the Boer farmers of South Africa against the British.

Laurier had to use all his political skill to engineer a compromise. In the end, a volunteer battalion, equipped and trained in Canada, was sent to South Africa under British responsibility. In total, some 7 000 Canadians volunteered to fight.

Laurier's compromise was accepted more in English-speaking Canada than in Quebec. The political consequences and price Laurier was eventually to pay soon became apparent: his protegé, Henri Bourassa, resigned from the Canadian Parliament and returned to Quebec to found the League Nationale. He became a force that was to contribute mightily to Laurier's defeat a decade later.

4.1.2   Imperial Affairs

The dispute over the Alaska Panhandle, and the Boer War, illustrated the growing problem of "organization" in the British Empire. Canada, under the terms of the BNA Act, could not act independently in foreign relations. Yet it was no longer willing to allow Britain, with its separate, and increasingly distinct, interests, to negotiate on its behalf. Gradually, Canada became more independent. It had established a High Commission in London by 1880, and established independent foreign commercial relations.

While the issue of autonomy within the Empire was emerging in Canada, an opposite movement toward Imperial union—a single parliament and a single defense and commercial policy—was also developing. Its chief spokesman was British colonial secretary, Joseph Chamberlain. At the first Imperial Conference in London in 1897, on the occasion of Queen Victoria's Diamond Jubilee, the notion of unity was largely sidestepped. In subsequent conferences, the issue was raised again and pressures grew. As the pre-World War I military build-up with Germany accelerated during the early years of the new century, the pressure on Canada increased to the point where Laurier had to compromise.

4.1.3   The "Tin-Pot" Navy

The growing crisis between Britain and Germany prompted a special Imperial Defense Conference in 1909. Canada, along with other

"Dominions", was asked to organize and maintain a navy. In one sense, this represented a victory for colonial autonomy in that the principle of separate defense forces was established. However, it did mean Canada's direct involvement in British defense policy.

Laurier presented his Naval Services Bill to Parliament in 1910. The bill provided for a small navy which would receive two British ships. The ships would be crewed by Canadians, but would be placed at the disposal of the British Admiralty in case of emergency. Laurier was again caught between English-speaking Canadians, who generally thought Canada's support of the Empire was too hesitant and too little, and Quebec, which again accused him of betrayal and selling-out his native province. This time, however, the opposition in Quebec was led by the articulate Henri Bourassa.

4.1.4 "Canada's Century"

"The 20th Century belongs to Canada" is a quotation generally ascribed to Wilfrid Laurier. That he never, in fact, said so should not detract from the spirit of confident optimism regarding Canada's growth and development seen during his period in office.

Canada participated fully in the trade boom of the late 19th and early 20th centuries. Canada had also become a magnet for foreign immigration—not simply, or even mainly, from the British Isles or the United States. Canada had, at last, also become attractive to foreign investment. As part of the British Empire, Canada was able to take advantage of the imperial trade preferences. It could also take advantage of the dynamic North American market. Although a "free-trader" at heart—as had been Macdonald—Laurier embraced the National Policy with enthusiasm. He now grasped the advantages, and more importantly, the opportunity of establishing a freer trade regime between Canada and the United States.

4.1.5 Reciprocity

Trade and commercial relations in general, and various tariff measures in particular have always been a central issue between Canada and the United States. In most instances, Canada has been the supplicant. The United States has traditionally rejected reciprocity or Canadian proposals for limited and selected trade liberalization. The United States has responded with proposals for complete economic—

sometimes political—unity. However in 1910, President William Taft, mainly for domestic political and economic reasons, suggested reciprocal tariff reductions. Canada responded quickly.

Rather than proceeding along the lines of an Anglo-American treaty, Canada suggested concurrent action by both legislatures. The United States obliged, and the finished agreement was ratified quickly by a special session of the U.S. Congress in the summer of 1910, and presented to the Canadian Parliament in January of 1911.

The issue of high tariffs has always been a political issue in Canada. While such tariffs provided some security for the country's fledgling industries, they also resulted in higher costs for producers and consumers. Outside of the country's manufacturing centre in Southern Ontario, pressure for tariff reduction had been growing in Canada. When the Laurier government presented the reciprocity agreement, they caught the Conservative Opposition by surprise. But the opposition within and without the House of Commons began to grow. Canadian industrialists feared for their market—and British industrialists feared the new American competition, as did railway investors. More important, however, was the "deal behind the deal"—the fear that it was merely a first step to complete economic and, eventually, political union. As the emotional debate developed, hardheaded businessmen and politicians began to defect from the Liberal Party. Eighteen powerful Liberals led by Clifford Sifton bolted from the party. Sir William Van Horne of the CPR simply demanded of his fellow businessmen "...bust this deal."

Finally, exasperated by the Tory filibuster in Parliament, the frustrated, but still confident, Laurier called a snap election.

4.1.6   The Federal Election of 1911

The Speaker of the U.S. House of Representatives helped neither Taft nor Laurier when he announced that the reciprocity agreement brought closer the day when one flag would fly over a single North American state. In Quebec, the main issue was not reciprocity, but rather Laurier's earlier "betrayal" of Quebec's interests represented by the Naval Services Act. Henri Bourassa joined with the Conservative Party, the erstwhile defenders of the Empire, to defeat Laurier. The Conservatives won 134 seats, 27 of them in Quebec, giving them an overall majority. The Age of Laurier—surprisingly and abruptly—was over.

CHAPTER 5

From Colony to Nation: The Great War

5.1 Robert Borden

Robert Borden became leader of the Conservative Party in 1901. Throughout the decade of his leadership in Opposition, he was over-shadowed by the flamboyant Wilfrid Laurier. He worked diligently, nonetheless, to rebuild the party's cohesiveness during the years of boom and growth. When he was thrust, somewhat surprised, into the office of Prime Minister, he was saddled with problems, particularly political debts he had to repay and the strange coalition he had cobbled together to win the 1911 election.

His government differed little in major policy matters from the administration he had replaced. His first initiatives—the expansion of Ontario and Quebec northward, as well as the expansion of Manitoba's boundaries to the 16th parallel—created little division within Parliament. However, by 1912, the economic boom was clearly over, and a new world-wide recession had begun to "bite." New immigrants searching in Canada for economic opportunities arrived only to swell the increasing ranks of the unemployed. The ecological problems associated with rapid agricultural development in the drought-prone south and central prairies (the Palliser Triangle) led to the first crop failure. Railway projects underwritten by the previous government now faced bankruptcy or bailout. Also, the contentious language issue arose again when Ontario passed legislation to restrict the teaching of French.

Borden also faced serious problems with the coalition he had built to defeat Laurier. These problems centered on Canada's relationship with the Empire, particularly the issue of contributing to the development of the Imperial Navy. While the election outcome did provide for a workable majority for the Conservatives, Borden did include, in minor portfolios, supporters of the Nationalistes from Quebec.

In Europe, the military and political situation had been greatly altered. Britain, now in alliance with its old rivals France and Russia, faced a rapidly strengthening and expansionist Germany. It was clear that Europe was heading toward war—a war, moreover, in which Britain would be vulnerable.

Shortly after his election, Borden visited Great Britain. In meetings with the brash, persuasive Winston Churchill, then First Lord of the Admiralty, Borden became convinced of the necessity of Canada contributing somehow to the naval rearmament of Britain. On his return to Canada, he proposed legislation in which Canada would contribute to building three British warships. This proposal caused one Quebec cabinet minister to resign, and a Liberal filibuster, which would drag on until 1913. Albeit finally passed by Parliament, the measure was defeated by the Senate. As war loomed in 1914, Canada watched, unprepared yet not uncommitted.

5.1.1 The Ontario Election of 1914

In Canada's early history, in most instances the explosive issue of language of education saw the word Catholic almost co-terminus with that of French. But that was not always the case. In Ontario, the focal point of the election of 1914 was the restriction of French education. Yet one of the key movers behind what became known as Regulation 17 was Michael Fallon, Roman Catholic bishop of London. While it was claimed that Fallon was motivated by a personal grudge against francophone co-religionists, the essential political reason was concern over increasing francophone migration into eastern Ontario.

Protestant, anglophone, and pro-empire, Ontario was the heartland of Borden's Conservative Party strength. The Conservative Premier of the province, James Whitney, gleefully called an election—in which the Liberal Opposition tried to vie with the

Tories in support of Regulation 17. The Conservatives won with a landslide. The message was not lost on Ontario's French minority, which saw only prejudice and betrayal. All French Canadians, within and without Quebec, received the same message. It was the eve of the Great War in which the issue of Canadian unity would be tested as seldom before.

5.1.2 The Empire Calls

The shot at Sarajevo which was "heard around the world" reached Canada on August 4, 1914. Germany had attacked France through neutral Belgium; and Britain—France's ally and long-time guarantor of Belgium neutrality—had declared war. The Governor-General was informed of this action by the Colonial Office in London, and Canada was thus at war. Parliament was quickly recalled. In a climate of militaristic euphoria, the Prime Minister announced that "...the manhood of Canada stands ready to fight beyond the seas...." Sir Wilfrid Laurier, now Leader of the Opposition, rose to declare, "...when the call goes out, our answer goes at once...'Ready, aye Ready.'" In the midst of this, Parliament passed The War Measures Act, an extraordinary piece of legislation which was to remain with Canada long after the war passed. For now, the Act gave the government power to prosecute the war without parliamentary constraints.

There is no question that in English Canada, the war and the defense of Great Britain released a large reserve of patriotism and national unity. Thousands of young men rushed to enlist or to join in the civilian war effort. By February 1915, the first Canadian division reached the trenches of France.

5.2 The Home Front

The enthusiasm for war that swept Canada in the summer of 1914 varied from province to province, from ethnic group to ethnic group, and between native born and naturalized citizens. There were recently arrived immigrants from the British Isles whose time in Canada had been spent mainly as unemployed. They saw the army as an opportunity to escape as well as an expression of love for the distant homeland. There were over 100000 recent immigrants from Germany and the Austro-Hungarian Empire, and another 400000 from associated countries, who were now considered to be "enemy aliens." These people faced not only questions of divided loyalties but were also confronted with open hostility and persecution. French Canadians—especially those living outside of Quebec—saw their cultural birthright challenged and threatened by an increasingly strident Anglo-Saxon majority. Even in Quebec, as pressures for assimilation grew, so did the sense of alienation.

Social, racial, and class divisions in the country as a whole had been widening as the boom of the first decade of the century gave way to the depression of the second. For a brief moment, it seemed as if these divisions would be swamped in a "sea" of a war-inspired national unity. Henri Bourassa, Quebec's leading nationalist politician, lent support to the war effort in the beginning. Even before Wilfrid Laurier was able to make his famous "ready, aye ready" speech, the Quebec paper *La Patrie* announced on August 5, "...there are no longer French Canadians and English Canadians...Only one race now exists, united by the closest bonds on a common cause."

However, as the war dragged on, it seemed to heighten and exacerbate every social, political, cultural, and institutional hurt in the country. For a time, it threatened the social fabric of the nation. In the crucible of the war, Canada changed permanently.

5.2.1 Independence and Empire

Under the original terms of the BNA Act, Canada was created as a self-governing colony of the British Empire. However, in matters of foreign relations, Britain was firmly in control. Almost immediately, Canada chafed under these constraints. In dealings with the United States, which were virtually the only external affairs Canada had, Canadians felt undercut by British indifference, or victimized by what appeared to be Britain's primary concern over its own relations with the United States. Nevertheless, in the pre-war years, Canada gradually assumed more control over its external affairs.

Slow progress towards autonomy would probably have satisfied both Macdonald and Laurier. They would have continued, on one hand, to politely resist pressures from some quarters in Britain for Imperial unity while, on the other hand, accepting the protection of the Empire and other economic advantages deriving from semi-colonial status. Borden was more prone to accept the blandishments of the Empire. The practical argument in favor of this approach grew as the German threat to the Empire increased. Yet, while Borden could see Canada as a partner sharing responsibility in the Empire, he also asserted Canada's right to share in making imperial foreign policy.

Borden pressed his viewpoint. Britain however, had no real intention of agreeing to any such devolution of power. There the issue stood at the outbreak of war. And there it remained in spite of Borden's consistent attempts to alter British intransigence and Canada's increasing important role in the fighting. Although Canada became a major participant in the war in terms of manpower and as a supplier of material and food, its soldiers fought as part of the British Army throughout, its colonial status mostly unchanged.

5.2.2 Economics of War

The outbreak of war quickly changed Canada's economic circumstances. The markets for Canada's traditional exports—minerals, forest products, and grains—expanded. The war also provided Canada with a long-term opportunity to expand its manufacturing sector—which had developed mainly to serve domestic needs—into a major component of Canada's exports. Airplanes, motorized vehicles, and munitions were all manufactured for export. A modern shipbuilding industry developed. During the years 1915–18, over 1 500 new factories were created in 90 different Canadian communities. For the first time, Canada's industrial output surpassed its agricultural output. The nation's economy was transformed into an industrial one.

5.2.3 Quebec

Except for the briefest of moments, the outbreak of war did little to promote unity between French and English Canadians. Everything tending to reinforce Quebec's minority status seemed to be highlighted. The early recruitment drives appeared to be directed by and to the anglophone population. The volunteer organizations which had led the campaign to strengthen the war effort in English Canada seemed to be otherwise occupied in Quebec. Quebec's attachments and loyalties were to Quebec. Even those francophones who admired the British legacy in Canada did not extend this respect to Europe or the Empire, which was far removed. Quebec's attachment to France had long been lost with France's abandonment of the continent in the

18th century. The later French Revolution had created a different society from the clergy-dominated Quebec of early 20th century.

As the war dragged on, and its costs increased, opposition to it grew. In Quebec, as in other parts of Canada, the human sacrifices demanded by the war effort became intolerable. More and more soldiers were required for the front, and eventually volunteers were not forthcoming in sufficient number.

5.2.4 The War and Racism

The notion that there were Canadians who, because of their birthright, were less loyal to the British Empire was not restricted to French Canadians. Indeed, in wartime Canada, the whole concept of "enemy alien" seemed to extend to anyone whose native tongue was not English.

Racial issues in Canada that included, but went beyond, the problem of English and French had long lain dormant below the surface veneer of Victorian gentility. Thousands of Chinese labourers had been imported to help in the construction of the railway. Incredible obstacles were then placed in their way of permanent settlement. These included the infamous "head-tax" on any Chinese who attempted to reunify their families or to settle. A so-called gentlemen's agreement had been reached with the Japanese government earlier to restrict Japanese immigration, and pressure was constantly applied to limit other Asian settlement. The war, in a sense, legitimized and broadened the racial exclusiveness which had been more or less covert before. "Enemy aliens" were now to be penalized systematically. They were fired from government jobs, and faced intimidation, such as the use of special identification cards and internment. Amid hysterical claims of Germans preparing to invade Canada from bases in Milwaukee, an old Canadian town of Berlin was forced to change its name to Kitchener.

5.2.5 The Canadian Army

Canada, with a new and increasingly heterogeneous population, did not have a military tradition. Indeed, Canada was traditionally considered to be a haven for deserters and military resisters from many parts of Europe. Yet when war came, a Canadian fighting force was quickly organized. The first call for volunteers in 1914 was for

25 000—three times the size of the Canadian contingent in the Boer war. In 1915, Prime Minister Borden pledged a force of 500 000. This goal was an ambitious one for a country with a population of less than 8 million, and only 1.7 million males between the ages of 20 and 39. It was clearly impossible to reach that goal if the army was to remain a volunteer force.

5.2.6 Conscription

As the war ground on and casualties increased, the number of volunteers decreased. By 1917, the number of new recruits fell each month behind the new casualty figures. The pressure on Borden increased from Britain and from sections of English Canada to introduce conscription. On May 18, 1917, Borden made the announcement to the House of Commons. Anti-conscription riots broke out in Montreal; and Borden tried to salvage the situation by asking Laurier to join in a coalition government. Laurier refused, not only for personal political reasons but also because he knew that if he were to join the government, he would be finished politically in Quebec. In any event, Laurier's support for the war was weakening. Laurier also was opposed to conscription in principle.

Borden's electoral mandate had expired by 1916. Parliament had agreed to a year extension, but refused Borden's request for a further extension. The outcome of the resulting election would determine Canada's continued participation in the war.

5.2.7 Extending the Franchise to Women

In 1916, a reform government was elected in Manitoba which extended the suffrage to women. This act—which reflected women's long and sometimes bitter struggle for equal rights—was also connected to deep social changes that had taken place during the war: women, in record numbers, had entered the labour force in occupations hitherto closed to them. Sensing the militant mood of women, Arthur Meighan drafted the Wartime Elections Act, giving the vote to women whose next-of-kin had or were serving in the army. The act also took away the vote from citizens native to enemy territories who had been naturalized since 1902. Meighan called it a "splendid stroke" to "...shift the franchise from the doubtful British or anti-British of the male sex and to extend it at the same time to our patriotic women..."

5.2.8   The Federal Election of 1917

Borden had every right to fear the outcome of the election and to wish it postponed. The conscription crisis had split the nation along its traditional fault lines. And with all the sacrifice and cost involved in prosecuting the war, Canada was still being largely ignored by the British. Moreover, the domestic war effort had seen its share of inefficiencies, corruption, and apparently government sanctioned profiteering. The end of the war was nowhere in sight.

The Wartime Elections Act had given soldiers a transferable vote, meaning that they could vote for any candidate in any constituency they pleased. This provision alone gave the government control over about 25 percent of the vote. "It would have been more direct and at the same time more honest," one Liberal stated, "if the bill simply stated that all who did not pledge themselves to vote Conservative would be disenfranchised."

Borden was able to convince a number of prominent Liberals to desert Laurier and to join in the proposed Unionist government. Laurier, abandoned by most of his English Canadian supporters, fought for a losing cause amid charges ranging from cowardice to virtual treason.

While there was scarcely any doubt about the election's outcome, the vote did express how divided the country had become. Laurier received over 75 percent of the vote in Quebec, and Borden's Unionists received almost as much support in English Canada—64 percent.

5.2.9   From Ypres to Vimy Ridge

Canadian troops were fully engaged in trench warfare from September 1915, and from that point fought in some of the bloodiest battles of the war. In one engagement alone, 77 000 Canadians were ordered to move their line a few metres forward; they did so at a cost of 24 029 casualties. Of all the battles Canadians participated in, none is remembered more than Vimy Ridge on Easter Monday 1917, fought uphill to capture the heavily fortified ridge.

For Canada and Canadians, the battle of Vimy Ridge has assumed almost mythic proportions. Several historians claim it was the battle that defined Canada as a nation. Participation in the war certainly did mark a turning point in Canada's national development. Canada, for instance, became a full member of the League of Nations.

But the war was costly. A small country of less than eight million people had 40 percent of its able-bodied men in uniform; 61 386 died and another 172 950 were wounded.

The war had other, social costs. In prosecuting the war at Britain's side, the precarious balance between English and French Canada—the basis of Confederation itself—was upset. This balance has yet to be recovered.

CHAPTER 6

Between Wars

6.1   Restless Labour

As industry grew and developed so did organized labour. At the turn of the century, there were less than 100 000 trade unionists. In the rapid pace of pre-war industrial development, the movement grew to about 143 000 and by the end of the war, trade union membership neared 378 000. There were several trade union centres in Canada. The main body was affiliated with the American Federation of Labour (AFL). There was a smaller Trades and Labour Congress, which was Canadian and based mainly among railway workers. In Quebec, the main union body was a Catholic syndicate.

For the most part, the union movement was made up of tradesmen organized along craft lines. The bulk of unskilled workers and those in new industrial facilities remained unorganized. There were many attempts to organize on an industrial basis, and various more militant groupings in the United States such as the Knights of Labour, the I.W.W. (International Workers of the World), and the Western Federation of Miners who entered Canada from time to time. But their efforts were largely defeated by hostile employers and governments.

Labour matters were at first of little concern to government, and jurisdiction was split between the federal and provincial levels. In the first years of the 20th century, the federal government organized a department of labour. William Lyon Mackenzie-King, at age 26, became the first Minister of Labour. King was neither an employer nor unionist but rather a social worker turned politician; it was his "social" approach which government used to mediate labour disputes. King was defeated with the Laurier government in 1911, and federal power passed to the more openly hostile Conservative government.

Most pre-war labour disputes ended in the defeat, often violent, of the trade unions.

6.1.1   The Winnipeg General Strike 1919

Throughout the war, the trade union movement grew rapidly. The Conservative government used the War Measures Act to ban some of the more radical labour organizations, such as the I.W.W., and later legislated against any strike activity. Wages remained relatively stable during the war, but began to decline in the post-war period because of inflation. In 1918, a brief general strike in Winnipeg won wage increases for municipal workers. In 1919, the O.B.U. (One Big Union), a militant break-away group from the AFL, organized a General Strike against the private sector in the same city. The strike began on May 15, 1919, and was followed by a series of strikes in other cities across the country. While the strikes in most other cities petered out, in Winnipeg some 30000 answered the strike call—many or probably most of whom were not even union members. Strikers took over control of the administration of the city. By mid-June the resolve of the strikers appeared to be weakening. At this point the federal government—claiming to fear a foreign-led insurrection—passed draconian legislation to break the strike. On June 15, a body of special police waded into a demonstration. In the ensuing riot, hundreds were arrested, the strike leaders charged with sedition, and the strike smashed. The rising tide of labour militancy was, for a time, checked.

6.1.2   Farmer Discontent

At the end of the war, a third of Canada's families continued to earn their living from farming. While the war had created an agricultural boom and had increased grain prices, the farmers grew disenchanted with the Unionist Government's lack of concern. They grew increasingly bitter as the government reneged on its promise to exempt young farmers from conscription and ignored demands for lower tariffs and freight rates. The price of grain fell 45 percent in the first post-war crop year.

In 1916, the Canadian Council of Agriculture was formed and began to formulate a coherent set of farmer demands—which it was to call the New National Policy. Along with the calls for lower tariffs—the opposite of the old National Policy—it made new policy demands, calling for a graduated income tax and the nationalization of transportation.

6.1.3   Ontario Provincial Election of 1919 and Its Aftermath

Canadian farmers had long maintained a strong tradition of political activism. In 1919, the United Farmers defeated the Conservative government in Ontario. This electoral success was followed by others in Alberta and Manitoba.

The victory in Ontario destroyed one of the remaining pillars of the Unionist government in Ottawa, and led directly to the foundation of the Progressive Party which was to contest the next federal election.

6.1.4   The Progressive Party

The principle spokesman for Western farmers was a Liberal politician, Thomas Crerar. In 1917, he left the Liberals to accept the post of Minister of Agriculture in the Unionist government. By war's end, increasingly uncomfortable with the continued high tariff policy, he led eight other former Liberals across the floor. Crerar's main intention was to rejoin the Liberals. However, given the electoral success in Ontario and increasing strength in the West, he agreed to lead a new third party, the Progressives.

6.1.5   Unionist Disarray

At war's end, the collapse of the coalition government was inevitable. The coalition had never been stable, having no substantial representation in Quebec; in English Canada, its members remained either Liberal or Conservative first. For his part, Robert Borden continued to chase the "wil o'the wisp" of some type of imperial executive while seemingly losing interest in domestic affairs. The government drifted along and it was not until 1920—after the Liberals had chosen a new leader and the Progressive Party had been formed—that Borden chose to resign in favour of another coalition leader.

6.1.6 The Death of Sir Wilfrid Laurier

By rejecting conscription and a place in the Unionist Government, Laurier gracefully accepted defeat and the thankless job of Leader of the Opposition. He also saved the Liberal Party. With the end of the war and the Unionist government's decline evident, Laurier was confident he would make a political comeback. So confident was he that the Liberal Party would be the vehicle for uniting Canada in the next general election—and inspired by the experience and spectacle of American political conventions—Laurier called for a Liberal convention in 1919, the first in Canada's history. But Laurier died on February 16, 1919, before the convention could be held. Preparations continued, and Canada's first political convention was held the following August.

6.1.7 William Lyon Mackenzie-King

The grandson of the famous Canadian rebel, William Lyon Mackenzie, was Sir Wilfrid Laurier's protege. As a young man, King became one of Canada's first civil servants. He helped organize the federal department of labour. At age 26, after winning election as a Liberal, he became the first Minister of Labour. He was defeated with the government in 1911 and travelled to the United States, where after a time he became a labour advisor to the younger Rockefeller. Remaining loyal to Laurier, he returned to Canada to contest the election of 1917, which he again lost.

In 1918, King published a book *Industry and Humanity*, which was a rather rhetorical presentation of the relationship of the individual with the new industrial society. In many ways, it was considered advanced for its time: it called for a form of workman's compensation and unemployment insurance. These labour reforms had already been introduced in Europe, but were considered radical in Canada. Thus came King's reputation as a reformer.

In spite of these credentials, King at 44 was considered by many to be too young and brash to succeed Laurier. Yet, given his loyalty to Laurier and his refusal to accept conscription, he was the sole contender acceptable to the large Quebec delegation at the leadership convention. King was elected leader on the third ballot.

6.1.8 Arthur Meighen

Arthur Meighen was elected by the Unionist caucus upon Robert Borden's resignation in 1920. Meighen was a hard working, brilliant cabinet minister in the Unionist government. He was also a man of strict conservative views and a rigid approach to politics and political opponents. Meighen had authored the War Measures Act, and had used it as Minister of Justice to ban some union organizations and to stifle anti-war sentiment. He was the main proponent of conscription, and he had also acted as the government's point man in crushing the Winnipeg General Strike. He was a rigid proponent of high tariffs.

Given all the problems of the Unionist cause, the postwar economy went into recession in 1920, and unemployment was shortly to reach 13 percent of the work force. Meighen was clearly the wrong man at the wrong time. Nevertheless, he renamed the party the National Liberal and Conservative Party, and called for an election campaign from September 1, to December 7, 1921, Canada's longest ever.

6.1.9 The Federal Election of 1921

It was quite unclear who would win the election. The country was divided regionally as never before. The Conservatives had lost their Ontario base; the West was in revolt against both parties; and outside of Quebec, the Liberal's were still in a shambles. In the event, the Conservatives won only 50 seats, the Liberals 115, and the Progressives won a surprising 65. William Lyon Mackenzie-King would become the new Liberal Prime Minister. But for the first time in Canadian history, there would be a minority government.

6.2 The Empire, The United States, and Canada

As the war had developed, the general bonds between the United States and Great Britain had often been strained. Canada found itself in the middle of many disputes between the two powers.

Even though the election of 1911 ended talk of reciprocity, economic relations between the United States and Canada grew apace. New York City had replaced London as the main source of Canadian borrowing, and Canada was increasingly seen a prime destination for American investment. By the time the United States entered the war, mutual defensive arrangements became practical and necessary. In early

1918, Prime Minister Borden went to the United States to appeal for U.S. action to redress Canada's large balance of trade deficit. He met with an enthusiastic response and was even moved to state in one of his speeches: "...the resources of the two countries should be pooled...that the boundary should have little or no significance." At one Imperial war conference, Borden even proposed that Canada should no longer be represented by the British Embassy in Washington but should be allowed its own diplomatic representation to facilitate joint American and Canadian affairs. At the time, little developed from this proposal.

In the immediate post-war period, relations between Canada and the United States developed along with the economic boom of the 1920s. Mackenzie-King, as we have seen, had always had close ties with the United States. In power, King's first priority in international affairs was to strengthen Canadian independence from Britain. He opposed closer imperial ties. He also established that Canada and the Canadian parliament would be the sole authority deciding on military issues, and he moved to establish some permanent diplomatic relationship with the United States.

6.3 King and Parliament

Throughout the following decade, Arthur Meighen would be King's nemesis in the House of Commons. Meighen, rigid and dogmatic, was also a brilliant debater who could verbally demolish the arguments of the more wordy Mackenzie-King. But King was the consummate politician, pragmatic and always open to compromise. These skills would be necessary for anyone about to lead the bitterly divided country. His years of practice as a labour conciliator, forging compromises while appearing to have no opinions of his own, stood him in good stead as he brought together conscriptionists and Laurier loyalists, imperialists and nationalists, reformers and reactionaries, all of whom were represented in a parliament split along regional lines.

King's move away from the Empire and imperial ties won favor in Quebec and among nationalists, but he was careful not to move too far to challenge the sensitivities of anglophiles. He reduced the external tariff to win the support of the Progressives—but not as much as to anger industrialists. He won support for his promise to institute an old age pension and other measures, which he postponed cautiously. The

Progressive Party was unable to provide any coherent opposition to the government. (King would often dismiss them as being merely "Liberals in a hurry".) And it soon became clear that Canada was heading again to a two party parliamentary system.

6.4   Prohibition

Most of Canada, like the United States, moved toward prohibition during the war and early post-war periods. However, it became clear within a few years that prohibition was not working: Quebec never enforced it, and by 1924 the idea was dead in just about every province. Prohibition spawned the bootlegging industry. Before the ban on alcohol was lifted, there was a thriving liquor trade to the United States from the French islands in the St. Lawrence and from the British Colony of Newfoundland. Once the ban was lifted in mainland Canada, "rum running" became an even greater export. This trade in liquor created many problems on both sides of the border, not least of which was the corruption it fostered within the Canadian Customs Department. Investigations into this department began in 1924.

6.5   Maritime Discontent

The Maritimes—and Nova Scotia in particular—were always dubious about Confederation. They now saw themselves as victims in the ongoing struggle between more powerful regional interests. There thus arose a demand for a new National Policy which would do for the Maritimes what the previous policy had done for the prairies and Ontario and Quebec. Specifically, Nova Scotia was concerned about the decline of its coal and steel industry: Central Canada was importing more U.S. coal and steel given the lower tariffs. A Maritime Rights Movement grew, demanding higher tariffs on steel and coal, subsidized freight rates, and other concessions. Meighen, despite the risk of alienating Ontario voters, supported these demands. Mackenzie-King, because of the risk of alienating Ontario, pretended not to hear the demands as the next election drew closer.

6.6   The Federal Election of 1925

Because he was able to co-opt most of the members of the Progressive Party as well as to maintain the Liberal base in Quebec, Mackenzie-King fully expected to be re-elected with a comfortable majority in 1925. This was not to be. The Conservative Party under Arthur Meighen's dogged leadership won 46 percent of the vote and the largest block of seats, 116. These gains came mostly from the Maritime provinces. The Liberals were reduced to 99 seats, and King was defeated in his own constituency. The Progressives were reduced to 24 members, most of who now called themselves "cooperating independents."

Despite his apparent defeat, Mackenzie-King refused to resign. He insisted on his right to meet Parliament and to seek the support of the remaining Progressives. Both he and Meighen met with the Progressives, but the latter threw their reluctant support to King who proceeded to direct the government from the visitor's gallery.

6.7   The Constitutional Crisis

As the new session began, King proposed sweeping reforms designed to please all factions of the fractured Parliament. His tactic appeared to be to get all of his legislative proposals passed and then to call another election. If this was his plan, it was stopped in its tracks by the report investigating corruption in the Department of Customs, which was tabled in the House. The report concluded that corruption was pervasive, all the way to the Minister of Customs. As the debate on the report began, it was soon clear that the government would lose a vote of confidence in the House and be forced to resign. Not only would this be a humiliation, but also a sure electoral defeat. King decided to move first and asked the Governor-General to dissolve Parliament and call a new election before the report could be voted upon. The Governor-General, Lord Byng, refused and Mackenzie-King resigned. Meighen was asked to form a government, but it was defeated shortly after it was formed. The Governor-General had no choice but to call an election.

King was overjoyed. Now he could fight an election not on charges of corruption and political patronage, but on independence and the sovereign rights of the Canadian Parliament. Whether Canada's long struggle for independence from the British Crown was at stake in the election is somewhat beside the point. Mackenzie-King was determined to make Canadians believe that it was. As he confided in his diary, "...I go into battle of another election believing we have an issue that the people will respond to."

He was right.

CHAPTER 7

Boom and Bust: The Boom

7.1 The New Politics of 1926

The federal election of 1926 gave the Liberal Party under Mackenzie-King a clear working majority. It reduced but did not destroy the Conservative Party, and independent candidates captured 20 seats. To casual observers, it would appear that the election returned Canada to politics as usual, with two viable federal parties alternating power. But politics in Canada had changed radically. While the main thrust of Macdonald, Laurier, and even Borden had been to create a strong federal government, Mackenzie-King's policies dealt more with brokering power between the regions, fundamentally weakening federal authority. This process was assisted by economic changes that tended to heighten regional disparities, and began to change the focus from east-west to north-south development.

7.1.1 Canada and the New Commonwealth

The transformation of the British Empire into the British Commonwealth was complete by 1926. The Commonwealth then was described as a group of "autonomous communities within the British Empire, equal in status, in no way subordinate to one another...united by a common allegiance to the Crown and freely associated as members of the British Commonwealth of Nations."

This document essentially described a state of affairs that had existed for several years. In fact, in 1927, Canada posted its first ambassador to Washington and quickly followed with appointments to

Paris and Tokyo. High commissioners were exchanged between Ottawa and London; and communications between the British and Canadian governments were handled by the respective commissions, bypassing the Governor–General.

7.1.2   The Economics of the Boom

The boom of the "Roaring Twenties" took hold in Canada as in the United States. Dance crazes and Hollywood movies, all associated with the "Jazz Age," came North. These cultural "imports" paralleled Canada's import of goods from the United States. Moreover, a branch plant industrial economy developed. Automobiles provide a good illustration. By the late 1920's, Canadian auto production exceeded 500,000 cars a year. This production was mainly in operations controlled by American corporate giants such as General Motors, Ford, and Chrysler. Half of this automobile production was for export, duty free, throughout the British Empire.

In agriculture and other staples, production also boomed. Canada now produced over two-thirds of the world's pulp. New mines opened, and close to 4,000 miles of railway track was laid to bring goods to market. Canada harvested 600 million bushels of wheat in 1928, the last year of the boom. Unfortunately this was 127 million more than the country could sell. "The end," as John Kenneth Galbraith was to remark, "was here, but it was not yet in sight."

7.1.3   Women's Rights

Women began receiving the vote during the war. Beginning in Manitoba and Alberta, the women's suffrage movement gradually succeeded in all provinces except Quebec during the 1920's. Some historians claim that the suffrage movement was less about women's issues than about Anglo-Saxon middle-class Protestant values, which were perceived to be under threat from the mass immigrations of the period.

The war saw women move into different occupations and struggle to open up various professions. The struggle for equality, moreover, continued after the war. The first female member of parliament in the British Commonwealth, Agnes MacPhail, was elected in 1921. Canada's first Women's Olympic contingent was sent to the 1928 games.

On October 18, 1929, an earlier Supreme Court judgement that women were not persons and therefore could not be appointed to the Senate was overturned by the Privy Council. The judgement read in part: "to those who ask why the word (person) should include females, the obvious answer is why should it not?" The judgement went on the state that "the exclusion of women from all public offices is a relic of days more barbaric than ours." Shortly after this judgement, Cairine Wilson was appointed to the Senate by Mackenzie-King.

7.2   The Fall and Rise of Mackenzie-King

Given Canada's close economic ties with the United States, the stock market crash of October 1929 was felt just as keenly in the markets of Montreal and Toronto as they were in New York. Canada's economy was geared to exports. Thus, Canada began to feel the economic crunch coming a year earlier as the world prices for Canada's staple exports began to fall. Between 1929 and 1933 income from exports dropped a ruinous 67 percent. Most of the wheat crop of 1928 was unsold. By the 1929 crop year, there was no market at all. Wheat, which typically sold for $1.69 a bushel was sold for under 30 cents a bushel, when it could be sold at all.

To make matters worse, there was drought and pestilence on the prairies. The top-soil of many parts of Saskatchewan was literally blown away. The income of the province's farmers fell 90 percent within two years.

While provinces like Saskatchewan suffered a devastating depression, other regions such as the Maritimes had never really shared the boom of the 1920's. But even in the industrial heartland, wages and working conditions had been declining throughout. Promised reforms such as unemployment insurance had never materialized, and when mass layoffs hit, the effects were felt immediately.

In a short time, provincial governments were going bankrupt trying to finance even meagre welfare programs. They began to appeal to the federal government for help. Help was not forthcoming, as Mackenzie-King looked upon the economic crisis as a political problem. He first tried the usual solutions of balancing the budget and slashing government expenditures. Many of the provincial governments appealing for federal help were led by Conservatives. In 1930, King, ever the politician, told the House of Commons: "As far as giving money out of the federal treasury to any Tory government in this country for these alleged unemployment purposes...I would not give them a five cent piece."

The "Five cent piece speech" was to haunt him through the next federal election campaign, when he and his government were defeated.

7.2.1 Foreign Policy

The 1920s marked Canada's coming of age as an independent nation. There were, however, several sources of pressure on Canada's emerging foreign policy. Isolationists, mainly in Quebec, rejected any foreign policy coordination through the League of Nations, just as they had opposed such coordination within the Empire. During the League's debate on "Article X" of the League Covenant calling for collective security against aggression, a speech by Canada's representative summed up the position: "Canada is a fireproof house, far from the source of any conflagration." This would represent Mackenzie-King's position entirely. King, whose main preoccupation was to keep the country together by bridging the faultline between English and French Canada, always felt that the essential pressures on Canadian unity came from external issues. He wanted an independent foreign policy, but that policy should reflect Canada's limited involvement with foreign matters. Within this approach, and not contradictory, at least in his own mind, King was determined to strengthen Canada's relations with the United States and the Americas in general. He wished to link Canada with the most dynamic power in the new world.

7.2.2 Constitutional Issues

Throughout the 1920s, several legal challenges to the federal government's authority by various provinces saw the latter gain increasing areas of jurisdiction. The decisions in turn led to provincial demands for a greater share of revenues. They also led to cost-sharing initiatives. An example of this was the Old Age Security system, which finally came into being in 1927. Costs were borne equally between the provinces and the federal government.

As the series of Empire conferences leading to the independence of the Dominions were finally resolved in the Statute of Westminster, Canada herself had to find a means of amending its own constitution. The first meeting of provincial and federal leaders to find an amending formula for the constitution was held in 1927. No agreement was reached. The British waited until 1931 to pass the Statute of Westminster, but Canada could not agree internally on an amending formula. Finally, Canada requested that her constitution remain in Britain, which it would until 1982.

7.2.3   The Conservative Return

While Mackenzie-King faced the Depression seemingly uncomprehendingly, Richard Bennett, an aggressive, hard-working millionaire lawyer from Calgary, had a plan. He would protect Canadian industry by raising tariffs. He would reorganize the British Commonwealth into a huge trading bloc: he would "…blast our way into the markets of the world or perish in the attempt." And perish he did. Within five years, Mackenzie-King was back in office. Nonetheless, Bennett's one term government was one of the most remarkable in Canada's history.

7.3   Richard Bennett: Federal Election of 1930

R.B. Bennett had been an active Conservative politician most of his life. While making his fortune both as a corporation lawyer for the C.P.R. in Western Canada as well as dabbling in real estate and other investments, Bennett was elected periodically to the federal parliament as well as to the newly established Alberta legislature. As a result of a long-time friendship with a prominent lumber and pulp magnate, E.B. Eddy and his wife, Bennett became heir to their fortune. This made him one of the wealthiest men in Canada. He succeeded to the leadership of the Conservative party at its first open convention in Winnipeg in 1927, and confidently began to develop a winning electoral platform for the 1930 federal election.

7.3.1   Bennett's Economic Revival Plan

The U.S. market was vital to Canada by the 1930s. Yet trade between Canada and the United States virtually halted because of the economic collapse, and was made even worse by the strong protectionist measures adopted by the American Congress. Bennett's early response was to raise Canadian tariffs to protect what he could of the domestic manufacturing industry. He also thought that new tariffs would force

Canada's trading partners to lower theirs. For the first months this had a brief positive effect, but the Canadian market was too small and too weak in the Depression for the measures to help.

Bennett's plan also included a redirection of trade to the British Commonwealth. He envisaged a huge trading bloc with high tariff walls against outsiders. To these ends, Bennett promoted an Imperial Economic Conference in Ottawa in 1932. While the conference did not live up to Bennett's expectations, he was able to negotiate several agreements with various members of the Commonwealth. But they were of little benefit given that the Depression was worldwide. Even in the best of circumstances, the Commonwealth could never make up for the loss of the American market. The Depression deepened.

7.3.2 Economic Experimentation

In the United States, Franklin Delano Roosevelt's first administration was beginning to experiment with new economic strategies deriving from the ideas of British economist John Maynard Keynes. Bennett, for all his efforts to provide some sort of relief to the unemployed as well as provide more funds to the provinces, was a very conventional economic thinker. He tried to wait out the Depression as if it were merely a self-correcting cyclical event. As the Depression deepened, his policies became more defensive and reactionary. Canadians responded to Bennett much as Americans did to Herbert Hoover. Yet Bennett was also quite a creative leader in some areas. He established the Bank of Canada to regulate the credit and monetary system. In 1932, he created the Canadian Broadcasting Commission (later to become the Canadian Broadcasting Corporation) to broadcast in both English and French and to protect and develop a Canadian communication system. He laid the groundwork for the creation of Trans-Canada Airlines, to ensure the development of an east-west transportation grid. The Canadian Wheat Board was also organized to control the sale and price of wheat. All these institutions were to be publicly controlled.

7.4   Radical Movements of the 1930s

Periods of crisis produce movements advocating radical solutions. In the 1930s, Canada, like every other industrial country, had various radical groups on the political left and right. In Canada, some of the most important groups reflected the traditional faultline in politics, the division between the English and French.

7.4.1 Union Nationale

In Quebec, a right-wing nationalist party, the Union Nationale, was formed, mainly from a rump group of Conservatives. Led by a charismatic figure, Maurice Duplessis, it took power in 1936. Its early program promised to end corruption in government and to establish social programs as well as "provincialize" some foreign owned properties. In power, Duplessis developed a more nationalistic policy— provincial autonomy—and became more openly right wing.

7.4.2 The British Columbia Liberal Party

In British Columbia, the Liberal Party was captured by T.D. Pattullo on a program of "Work and Wages." It won the provincial election of 1935 and enacted programs which closely followed the New Deal legislation in the United States. Pattullo built a huge provincial debt, which he insisted Ottawa pay for without any strings attached. This also brought British Columbia into direct conflict with the federal government.

7.4.3 Social Credit in Alberta

In Alberta, another movement developed based upon some obscure monetary theories of an English engineer, Major Douglas. This Social Credit Party captured power in Alberta in 1935, but after a brief, half-hearted, fling with the theories of Major Douglas, it quickly became a more traditional Conservative Party.

7.4.4 The "Red Tories"

While it would be wrong to suggest that any variety of the socialism is indigenous to Canada, the nature of early Canadian immigration as well as frontier conditions produced some forms of radicalism unique to Canada. This is reflected in a certain type of conservativism called Red Toryism. This view is basically conservative in its strong emphasis on the community. In practical political terms, it reflects, nonetheless, a view that is not hostile to government, or of government intervention in the economy. There are historical reasons for this, stemming from the peculiar development of Canada as a small country sharing a long border with a richer and more powerful neighbour. Also, in the 19th century, the Government itself had helped create an all-Canadian rail line. In the 20th century, R.B. Bennett did not hesitate to use the government and to insist on such ownership and control of other nationally important areas such as broadcasting, air transportation, and even film production. The Conservative Party, from the days of John A. Macdonald, has had close and important ties with sections of the labour movement.

In the 1930s, this strain in the Conservative Party was best reflected in H.H. Stevens, an important cabinet minister in Bennett's government. He grew increasingly disenchanted with the Canadian business elite during the Depression as well as with the government itself, whose main base of support was in this elite. Stevens was to later bolt from the government and to form his own unsuccessful Reconstruction Party.

7.4.5 The Cooperative Commonwealth Federation (C.C.F.)

In Canada, there is also a much more radical tradition related closely to sections of Protestantism, espousing a highly moralistic system of Democratic socialism.

One of the key figures of the Winnipeg General Strike of 1919 was a Methodist minister, J.S. Woodsworth. He was elected to Parliament in the subsequent federal election where he sat variously as a labour-independent or leader of a so-called Ginger Group. In the years of the Depression, this socialist ideal, now linked with the more traditional strains of Western European socialist ideas, became a political party. The C.C.F. was formed in 1932. In a convention at Regina, Saskatchewan in 1933, the party elected J.S. Woodsworth as its leader. The party advanced a program named the Regina Manifeso, calling for the nationalization of the key sectors of Canada's economy and a full program of social welfare legislation.

7.4.6 Bennett's New Deal

As R.B. Bennett entered the fifth year of his mandate, it was clear that none of his ad hoc measures were working. The economic and social situation grew worse. In the United States some of the New Deal policies were taking hold; and Bennett, at last, visited Washington and met with President Roosevelt. Upon his return he bought with his personal funds air time on the national radio service and delivered a series of speeches declaring his conversion to Keynsian economics and the New Deal. He announced a whole reform package, which stunned most of his listeners. A so-called "left" in his party, led by a maverick minister H.H. Stevens, had already bolted. They considered the reform proposals to be an insincere election ploy. And those who had been radicalized during the economic crisis considered his reforms too little and too late. The mainstream of the Conservative Party was still wedded to traditional economic policies and had no faith in the Roosevelt New Deal and wanted no part of it in Canada. This section of the party was furious at what they considered to be Bennett's betrayal.

Thus R.B. prepared to face the Canadian electorate, politically crippled by opposition in his own party.

7.5   King in Opposition

Mackenzie-King spent the years of Bennett's government as leader of the Opposition. His defeat in 1930 was probably the best political stroke of luck he could imagine, because while in opposition there is little to suggest that he had any better ideas than R.B. Bennett. King could sit back and watch Bennett's legislative proposals fizzle out. The government was being attacked by an aggressive Left and the political Right had also declared war on the Prime Minister. The premier of Quebec, Alexandre Taschereau said that Bennett had "launched into a Socialistic venture bordering on Communism."

7.6   The Federal Election of 1935

The election of 1935 produced the most lopsided majority in history. The Liberals gained 173 seats and the Conservatives were reduced to 40. The election also pointed to a serious problem with a number of parties competing in a "first past the post" electoral system. Thus, for instance, the Social Credit Party received 17 seats (reflecting their strength in Alberta), while the C.C.F. gained six seats despite receiving twice as many votes (albeit spread across Canada). H.H. Stevens and his Reconstruction Party captured one seat.

CHAPTER 8

The War Years

8.1 Wartime Economy

Mackenzie-King's good fortune in being defeated just as the Great Depression deepened continued: his re-election occurred just as the economy began to show signs of a recovery. King moved swiftly to conclude negotiations with the United States, which R.B. Bennett had begun. These led to a reduction in tariffs between the two countries. He also moved to test the legality of his predecessor's "New Deal" legislation. While the Supreme Court of Canada upheld most of the legislation, a further appeal to the British Privy Council ruled against Bennett's legislation. This ruling—consistent with earlier judgements of the Privy Council—broadened the powers of the provinces while restricting those of the federal government. It illustrated the need to adapt the constitution to fit the 20th century needs of a modern state.

8.1.1 The Rowell-Sirois Commission

The ruling of the Privy Council forced the federal government to find a way to balance federal/provincial jurisdictions. The Rowell-Sirois Royal Commission was established in 1937. It took the commission three years to produce its final report. By which time the country was at war and the federal government had assumed extensive emergency powers.

The commission recommended that the federal government be given exclusive power to collect direct taxes. In return, the federal government had to make subsidies available to the provinces to maintain minimum standards of welfare and social services. This principle became the basis of the equalization formulas as Canada later developed its social services. Although the thrust of the report was based on and directed at social assistance and the removal of regional inequalities, the wartime emergency had already given these powers to the federal government. This did not stop the larger provinces such as Ontario, Quebec, and British Columbia from refusing even to discuss the report with the federal government.

In 1940, a constitutional amendment was passed giving the federal government the power to establish a national unemployment insurance scheme. With the wartime boom beginning, the scheme was hardly needed, but it did set a legal precedent for future social welfare initiatives.

8.1.2   The Crown Corporation

The Liberal government transformed the Canadian Broadcasting Commission into the Canadian Broadcasting Corporation, creating a powerful broadcasting network in both English and French. The device was, in fact, a crown corporation. Such a corporation operated independently (at arm's length) of the government but was owned by, and often operated in a field regulated by, the government. Another crown corporation established was the Trans Canada Airlines. These corporations arose not from any enthusiasm for public enterprise, but from nationalist pressures to maintain and develop new forms of transportation and communications firmly in Canadian hands when the private sector was either unable or unwilling to do so.

This form of public enterprise was to grow during the war and post-war period, substituting for private enterprise in high risk or high capital ventures. These new corporations rose to meet the needs of the war effort and later to facilitate post-war economic reconstruction.

8.1.3   The Coming of the C.I.O.

Almost from its beginnings, the Canadian trade union movement has been associated with its American counter-part. Just as industrial organization began in U.S. factories through the Congress of Industrial Organizations (C.I.O.), so was the C.I.O. active in Canada. In 1937, the C.I.O. affiliate, the United Automobile Workers, achieved a significant breakthrough with a victorious "sit-in" strike at the General Motors plant in Oshawa, Ontario. Although this movement faced bitter opposition from employers and the Ontario government, it soon swept through the industrial heartland of Ontario and into the mines and basic resource industries throughout the country.

8.2   Canada at War

The signs of economic recovery in 1937 did not materialize and the depression, now compounded by prairie drought, continued. The government blamed international events and continued its cutbacks. However, increasing international tensions—the Italian invasion of Ethiopia, Japanese invasion of China, the civil war in Spain, and Germany's increasingly strident demands—turned public attention to the threat of a new world war. The Canadian government, believing that nothing tore at the country's fragile internal unity than international issues and involvements, supported Western appeasement. Even when war came, Canada sought a "limited liability."

8.2.1   The Wartime Election

Great Britain declared war on Germany and the Axis powers on September 3, 1939. Canada, now totally autonomous, summoned Parliament. Anticipating war, the government invoked the War Measures Act and began recruiting soldiers. Parliament met the following week and declared war on September 10. Even with the declaration of war, Mackenzie-King remained cautious about Canada's commitment. King, ever mindful of the mistakes of Borden and Laurier during the last war, tried to please all sections of the country—including the promise never to invoke military conscription for overseas duty.

In Quebec, the nationalist Premier, Maurice Duplessis, called an election, portraying himself as a defender of Quebec interests against Ottawa and raising again the fear of conscription. He was soundly defeated.

In Ontario, King was under attack for being too half-hearted in the war effort. The premier of Ontario, Mitch Hepburn, pushed a resolution through the Ontario Assembly criticizing King's cautious war effort. In the face of this attack, King summoned Parliament again, defending the government's actions in the speech from the

Throne. He then dissolved the House for a federal election. The opposition was caught by surprise. On March 26, 1940, King won the greatest political landslide in Canadian history, winning 181 seats out of a total 245.

8.2.2 Canadian/American Relations

Canadian/American relations had improved steadily during the late 1930s. Roosevelt and Mackenzie-King developed a warm personal relationship. Two successive trade liberalization treaties were negotiated; and as war loomed, the relationship strengthened to the point that, at a speech in Kingston in 1938, Roosevelt virtually guaranteed Canada's military security.

8.2.3 The War Changes

The period called the "Phoney War" came to a shattering end in April 1940, when Hitler attacked Norway. Within weeks, the Nazi "Blitzkrieg" swept across Western Europe. By June 4, the British army escaped the Continent at Dunkirk and on June 12, Churchill declared, "...the Battle of France is over; the battle of Britain has begun."

For Canada, everything had now changed. There was no more talk of limited involvement. Canada's response was now total: it had to raise several more divisions; it had to build a navy to escort convoys across the Atlantic; and it had to build its own aircraft and develop its own defense procurement infrastructure. Canada had little experience, no training, and had to find millions of dollars in loans.

8.2.4 Ogdensburg

In mid-August 1940, President Roosevelt was in upstate New York to review a regiment of the National Guard. He contacted Mackenzie-King to join him. King travelled virtually alone to Ogdensburg; and in an informal meeting with the American president, he signed the "Ogdensburg Agreement" establishing a permanent Joint Board of Defense that would effectively establish a joint and single defense of the "north half of the western hemisphere." This agreement outlived the war, and became the basic defense document governing relations between Canada and the United States ever since. The agreement was signed without any reference to either Parliament or Congress.

King signed the Ogdensburg agreement in the belief that the treaty brought two great English-speaking powers together. Winston Churchill was under no such illusions. Ogdensburg represented, in his mind, Canada's transfer from one empire to another. However, Churchill—who had promised that he would not "preside over the dissolution of the British Empire"—was in no position to complain. Ogdensburg made possible Canada's role as supplier of food and war materiel to Britain during its darkest hour in World War II.

8.2.5 Natural Resources Mobilization Act

This act enabled the government to mobilize, ration, and allocate all Canada's human and natural resources. Canadians over 16 years of age registered, and could either be conscripted for industry—"frozen" in their jobs—or for military service. The government initially maintained its promise that any overseas army would be strictly volunteer, even though this, in effect, created two armies.

8.2.6 C.D. Howe: Minister of Munitions and Supply

The most dynamic figure in the total war effort was not Mackenzie-King, but C.D. Howe, Minister of Munitions and Supply. Howe, an American-born engineer and businessman, was first elected in 1935. Howe created the Crown Corporation, the C.B.C., and organized air transportation. He also placed Canada's harbours under efficient federal control. In war, he took complete control of the Canadian economy, presiding over the massive war-time expansion. He did this by tax concessions, massive direct investments, and huge government borrowing. As the Canadian economy grew, the government raised taxes six-fold and borrowed over $12 billion, mostly from individuals. By 1943, 1.2 million Canadians were working in factories, most of which had not existed in 1939. Howe justified such massive borrowing—and his lack of concern over the consequences of the sweeping restructuring of federal/provincial fiscal arrangements—by saying, in effect, if we win, who will count the cost, and if we lose, who will care?

In the first two years of the war, inflation rose to over 15 percent. Howe then instituted price and wage controls, which kept the rate at three percent until the end of the war.

The costs of wartime production were reflected in Canada's exports. Before the United States entered the war, Canada was the major allied supplier, with two-thirds of Canada's war production being exported. This caused a serious problem for Canada early on, as machinery and tools had to be purchased mainly in the United States. The deteriorating Canada/U.S. trade balance resulted in a serious decline in the Canadian dollar.

8.2.7   The Hyde Park Agreements

Previous defense agreements with the United States enabled Canada to supply the embattled British. Moreover, Roosevelt did everything possible to evade, even subvert, American neutrality laws to support Britain. However, it soon became clear that Canada's war effort required more tangible American economic help. The Hyde Park Agreements were a result of negotiations at the estate of the American President in April 1941. Among other things, the agreements called for American purchases of $250 million of Canadian munitions. This ceiling was soon raised. They also provided for material sent to Britain be paid for out of Lend-Lease arrangements, and out of British funds frozen in American accounts. The agreements also led to increased American purchases of Canadian goods, which helped redress the bilateral balance of payments problem.

8.2.8   Canadian Military Participation

The Canadian division in England was soon reinforced. Furthermore, the Canadian army was the backbone of the ill-fated Dieppe raid; Canada also dispatched troops to defend Hong Kong. A Canadian navy was created to guard mainly the convoys to Britain. The Canadian air force played a role in the later stages of the war, and many Canadians served in the Royal Air Force (R.A.F.).

However, compared to the role played in the previous war, many Canadians, unjustly it seems, felt that Canada's participation was rather lacklustre.

As military engagements grew, casualties mounted, and after the United States and the Soviet Union joined the war, the demand for overseas conscription arose. Mackenzie-King hesitated and procrastinated, stating: "conscription if necessary, but not necessarily conscription." Faced on the one side with memories of the split with Quebec during the last war and, on the other side, with the need and clamour for conscription—which threatened to split the government—King agreed to hold a plebiscite. The vote split the country with English Canada voting solidly for conscription and Quebec voting even more solidly against. Conscription for overseas service was finally enacted, and some conscripts actually saw service in Europe.

Meanwhile, as the pace of war increased and the tide gradually turned, Canadians participated in nearly every major campaign and theatre of war. At the war's end, Canada was the world's fourth largest military power, after the United States, the Soviet Union, and Britain.

CHAPTER 9

The Postwar Boom, The Prelude

9.1 Wartime Politics

During the war years, the industrial trade union movement grew very rapidly in Canada. On the prairies, the cooperative movement revived. The Cooperative Commonwealth Federation (CCF), which sought to combine the agrarian socialist movement with the new industrial union movement, won only eight seats in the 1940 federal election. However, within a year, it had reorganized itself. Replacing its founder, J.S. Woodsworth, with a Saskatchewan school principal, M.J. Coldwell, it revitalized itself and won an important federal by-election in 1942. In the Ontario election of 1943, it won 34 seats—only four seats less than the victorious Conservatives. In 1944, it won power in Saskatchewan.

The country's leftward political shift, was noted by the Conservative Party, which was shortly to change its name, its leader, and its policies. In Ottawa, Mackenzie-King began planning his post-war political strategy as early as 1942. He advanced a Charter of Social Security.

9.1.1 A Federal By-Election of 1942

After his resignation as Conservative leader in 1927, Arthur Meighen retired to the Senate, where he watched the Conservative election debacles of 1935 and 1940. In 1942, the leaderless Conservatives convinced Meighen to lead them again. He tested his leadership in a by-election in Toronto and lost to the CCF candidate. Meighen, once again, quickly retired, and a leadership convention was called for later that year.

9.1.2 The Port Hope Conference

In the wake of Meighen's Toronto defeat, a group of younger Conservatives met in the town of Port Hope, Ontario, to develop a new Conservative policy they hoped would bring them out of the political "wilderness." The participants, known as the Port Hopefuls, developed a program including many Conservative dogmas such as support for free enterprise and conscription, etc. Yet the charter also included more "radical" goals, such as full-employment, low-cost housing, trade-union rights, as well as a whole range of social security measures, including a government financed medicare system.

9.1.3 The Conservatives Become Progressive Conservatives

While many members of the Conservative establishment rejected the Port Hope Charter, the essence of the charter pervaded the following leadership convention. Delegates at the convention drafted the long-time Premier of Manitoba, John Bracken, as leader. He was not even a member of the party. Bracken supported the Port Hope Charter and insisted that the party register this policy shift by changing its name to the Progressive Conservative Party.

9.1.4 Liberals Plan the Post-War Welfare State

When he was elected leader of the Liberal Party in 1919, Mackenzie-King carried the aura of a reformer. He had recently published a book, *Industry and Humanity*, which proposed several social welfare measures. In office, however, King was a conventional, cautious leader—and the promises of 1919 were largely unfulfilled. Yet by the 1940s, King moved to implement a comprehensive, universal social policy. In 1940, an unemployment insurance plan was developed, which was further extended in 1945. The old age pension was extended and increased. Plans were also developed for veterans' housing, educational grants, farm assistance programs, and retraining provisions. Even more ambitious medicare and pensions schemes were promised. While many of these latter ideas required long and complicated federal/provincial negotiations, there was one program which was quick and entirely within federal jurisdiction—the "Baby Bonus." Every month, every family would receive a cheque from the federal government based upon the number of family members.

Critics argued that the scheme was based on pure political cynicism, others considered it to be a bribe to the more fecund Quebec. Supporters called the Baby Bonus needed support for the family as well as a sound economic measure (as it directly increased the spending power of all Canadian families). Coincidentally, the federal election was held a few days after the first cheque arrived at every Canadian family's household.

9.1.5   1945 Federal Election

Although losing some seats, Mackenzie-King's Liberals remained securely in power. The CCF almost tripled its seats from 8 to 28, capturing almost 17 percent of the vote—a percentage that has remained remarkably stable since. King had perceived shrewdly that his main threat came from the left, the CCF. In the pre-election period, he had thus pre-empted their appeal by moving the Liberal Party left in order to be a solid alternative to the socialists.

9.2   The Boom

As Europe and Asia lay in ruins, North America emerged from the war wealthy and strong. The war had resulted in much economic and military integration. Both Canada and the United States were determined to maintain and even encourage further integration. Canada had become a magnet for American investment in raw materials, now in short supply in the United States. Canada was also increasingly seen as an industrial and commercial partner. Canadian policy well suited and encouraged these aims.

9.2.1   C.D. Howe: "Minister of Everything"

C.D. Howe, whose brilliant organization of the wartime economy built an impressive industrial infrastructure, now set out as Minister of Reconstruction to adapt to a new peacetime role. His first priority was to ensure that the conversion to peacetime production did not repeat the experience after World War I, when, after a burst of economic activity to meet consumer demand, inflation resulted, followed by recession.

Reconstruction planning involved the transfer of factories back to orderly civilian production, meaning, in some cases, virtually giving them away to private owners. Many of these new owners would be American firms looking for facilities to meet increased U.S. demand. In areas where private investment could not be found, the existing crown corporation would be maintained. Howe, who was somewhat skeptical of the various social welfare measures proposed by his government—insisting instead that the best social program was full employment—worked tirelessly to convert the economy.

Howe was assisted by the growing political links between Canada and the United States, as the Cold War began and rearmament loomed. Canada was also a direct beneficiary of the American Marshall Plan, becoming a supplier of goods and services for rebuilding the European economies.

9.2.2   The Economic Miracle

In 1948, at Canada's initiative, free trade discussions began with the United States. The Canadian negotiators had few illusions about what such an agreement—even a complete customs union—would mean to Canada's independence, its relationship with the British Commonwealth, and even the traditional east-west axis upon which the country had been built. However, in most minds, the economic benefits outweighed the costs. The discussions began in secret and were concluded quickly. What happened next is still a matter of speculation. Mackenzie-King, now tired, disturbed, and disappointed with the development of the cold War, had read an editorial in *Life* magazine by Henry Luce—whom he hated—calling for just such a customs union as had been secretly negotiated. He had also read disturbing articles in other American magazines which had begun calling Canada the 49th state. He saw visions of his old mentor, Sir Wilfrid Laurier, brought down in 1911 by a much weaker and limited agreement with the United States. King, still very much in charge of the government, and capable, as always, of quick decisive action, changed his mind, tore the agreement up and ordered all the papers destroyed.

If free trade and a customs union was to be a dead issue for several decades, the process of economic integration continued apace. This integration meant huge development projects in almost every region of the country.

In 1947, oil was discovered in Alberta. Further exploration indicated huge reserves of both oil and gas. Prior to the 1940s, Canada had been almost totally dependent on imported oil, but it was soon to be self-sufficient. Within a decade, it was a net exporter of oil.

If at first Canadians were too busy enjoying their new found wealth and prosperity to notice the cost in the loss of ownership and control, they could hardly be blamed. Most accepted C.D. Howe's assertion that a dollar has no nationality. Canada remained a full partner in the booming North American economy of the early 1950s.

9.2.3   The Weakening Ties with Britain

Throughout the first post-war decade, Canada moved—in many cases symbolically—towards severing colonial ties. In 1947, a separate Canadian citizenship was created. In 1949, the Supreme Court of Canada became the final court of appeal. The BNA Act remained in effect to cover only some federal/provincial issues still unresolved by Canadian politicians. In 1952, the last British Governor-General retired, and Vincent Massey became the first Canadian Governor General. In 1949, the remaining colony in British North America, Newfoundland, voted narrowly to join Confederation, thus fulfilling the vision and plan of 1867.

Post-Confederate Canada

Entered Confederation 1867
Entered Confederation before 1900

BRITISH COLUMBIA 1871
ALBERTA 1905
SASKATCHEWAN 1905
MANITOBA 1870
YUKON TERRITORY
NORTH-WEST TERRITORIES

To Manitoba 1881
To Manitoba 1912
To Ontario 1912
To Ontario 1889
To Quebec 1896
To Quebec 1912

ONTARIO
QUEBEC
NEW BRUNSWICK
NOVA SCOTIA
P.E.I. 1873

Newfoundland and Labrador Joined Canada 1949

9.2.4 Igor Gouzenko

In a matter of weeks after the conclusion of World War II, a cipher clerk at the Soviet embassy in Ottawa asked for political asylum. The clerk, Igor Gouzenko, had documents indicating the existence of a Soviet spy ring in Canada. Moreover, since Canada had been the site of some of the early atomic experiments and scientists from several nations had lived and worked in Canada throughout most of the war, Gouzenko's revelations indicated the existence of spy rings in both England and the United States. The Gouzenko case was to greatly increase Western suspicions of the Soviet Union. It thus contributed in part to early Cold-War tensions.

9.2.5 International Commitments

Canada, a charter member of the United Nations, argued in the early stages of the U.N. for a distinct role for smaller and middle powers outside of the power blocs, which were then quickly forming. But Canada also accepted the reality of post-war politics, and quickly saw the need for a defense alliance that would extend America's defense line to Western Europe. Louis St. Laurent, Minister of State for External Affairs, was one of the chief exponents of the North Atlantic Treaty Organization (NATO). Indeed, Canadian troops were shortly to participate in the joint defense of Europe.

The Canadian view of NATO was somewhat more comprehensive than that of the United States, which saw it almost exclusively as a military alliance. Canada wanted to develop NATO into a broader international network which would include economic, social, and cultural functions. While the other nations paid more or less "lip service" to this broader concept of NATO, the Canadian ideal was largely stillborn.

The Canadian position in international affairs consistently supported the Western Alliance, including service abroad and joint defense of the North American continent—which later evolved into the North American Air Defense (NORAD). It also sought a constructive, independent role for itself.

In a search for a more independent role in foreign affairs, Canada participated in the Colombo Plan in which the more highly industrialized countries of the British Commonwealth would aid economic development of the weaker ones.

Canada participated in U.N. military action on the Korean peninsula and contributed a brigade to the fighting. And in 1954, Canada became part of an international team to observe the cease-fire agreement in Indo-China (Vietnam).

9.2.6   Louis St. Laurent

In 1948, Mackenzie-King retired. Although the party went through the ritual of a leadership convention, King made sure his trusted heir, Louis St. Laurent, succeeded to the leadership and the Prime Minister's office.

St. Laurent was a wealthy Quebec lawyer who came late to politics. As King's Quebec Lieutenant, he was successively Minister of Justice and later External Affairs. In the latter position, St. Laurent was the prime figure behind Canada's increasingly tight foreign and defense alliance with the United States.

St. Laurent quickly became a popular figure, and was soon dubbed "Uncle Louis." He proved to be a capable administrator. The government was labelled in the popular press as "Canada Ltd.", with St. Laurent as Chairman of the Board, and C.D. Howe as CEO.

9.2.7   George Drew and the Federal Election of 1949

The fourth leader of the Progressive Conservative Party since Mackenzie-King defeated R.B. Bennett in 1935, was Colonel George Drew. Although a successful premier of Ontario, Drew was perceived on the federal level as a rigid, old fashioned, and somewhat irrelevant anglophone Tory. The Liberal's swept back into power with their fourth straight victory.

9.3   Population Growth

The early post-war years saw rapid growth in population. In 1945, the population was almost 12 million. By 1961, there were 18 million Canadians. While much of the growth can be attributed to immigration—between 1945 and 1965 there were almost 2 million immigrants—most growth came from the natural birth rate. In what was to become known as the baby boom, Canada's birth rate soared to among the highest in the world—to 26 new children per 1 000 population per year.

9.4   The Mega-Projects

The 1950s abounded with huge industrial, transportation, and energy projects. The Trans-Canada highway began in 1948, and would cost over $1 billion before completion. Roads and railway lines were built to resource-rich areas, and whole new industries were developed— potash, asbestos, aluminum, and iron are in Ungava.

The new transportation technology of the 1950s, pipelines, developed to take Alberta oil to market. Large-scale hydro projects, such as Churchill Falls in Labrador and the Columbia diversion in British Columbia, Oregon, and Washington State were built. Joint hydro development between New York and Ontario accompanied the construction of the St. Lawrence Seaway.

The Seaway—a dream of Canada's for several decades, which would open the continental heartland to deep-sea navigation—had been opposed successfully by regional political interests in the United States. By 1952, Canada was ready to go it alone. This determination finally brought the United Sates along as a partner, and construction began in 1954.

Moreover, a national television service in both French and English was announced in 1952.

9.5   The American Takeover

The great economic success story of the decade was the development of the Alberta oil fields. However, ownership and control of the industry had passed almost completely into American hands. This could be said about almost every other aspect of the Canadian economy. One-half to three-quarters of Canadian industry was owned by American interests, and just about every one of the huge resource development projects were either financed (and owned) by American interests, or were joint ventures with Canadian interests—usually junior partners.

Canadian trade patterns also altered during this period, as the United States became almost the sole supplier and customer of Canada. Upwards to three-quarters of Canadian exports and imports were cross-border.

Canada also felt increasing cultural penetration, as films and magazines were almost exclusively American (albeit in Quebec, the language barrier worked against the mass importation of American culture). Before the C.B.C. was formed, early television meant tuning antennas to American stations, just as with radio. When the C.B.C. moved also to television broadcasting in 1952, instead of developing a distinct Canada system as had happened in radio, programming gradually became dominated by the American networks.

With Canada's defense system totally integrated with the U.S. one, and foreign policy between the two countries ever more closely aligned, the issue of economic dependency emerged gradually as a political issue. In the first years of the 1950s, the issue was almost a marginal one among minor left-wing groups, but it would not remain so.

9.6   The Government Party

Elected in 1935, the Liberal Party held office through the most protracted period of growth in Canadian history. In this time, the size of government grew and the scope of its activities expanded beyond recognition. The government began to function as if it were somehow apolitical, and was really merely administering society. The relationship between politicians and civil servants blurred. The question would be asked: are all civil servants Liberals, or are all Liberals civil servants?

One historian described the relationship as, "…civil servants and Liberal politicians were simply two divisions of the same armed forces— different members of a large, rapidly growing and extremely happy family. Government by party had virtually ceased to exist."

9.7   The Federal Election of 1953

Louis St. Laurent had recently turned 70 and was thinking much about retiring. But the party had not yet even thought of grooming a successor. After a postponement for the coronation of Queen Elizabeth, an election was called for August 1953. By all accounts, it was a listless affair with St. Laurent playing his favourite role of the rich, benevolent uncle of the large and happy Canadian family. The outcome was predictable. While a few Liberal seats were lost, the party's percentage of the popular vote remained the same.

9.8 Business as Usual

There was nothing in the outcome of the 1953 election to indicate any change of course or direction. But there were signs of stress and change in just about every other area. The government stood aloof and aside, continuing to manage the economy. It even declared two budgetary surpluses.

9.9 The Cold War

The war in Korea had ended in stalemate, and the goal of a united, free, and independent Korea faded. Canada was constantly searching for some independent role and thus often chafed at being "shunted aside" by the United States and Great Britain. Lester Pearson, until he was to play his role in Suez Crisis and Cyprus, gained a reputation in Washington and London as something of a nuisance. Secretary of State Dean Atcheson on at least one occasion denounced Pearson's "...crazy...moralistic interference..."

9.10 Arts and Letters

With all its growth, economic development, and urbanization, Canada remained very much a cultural backwater. The CBC and the National Film Board provided an outlet—indirectly subsidizing the creative arts—but Canada had generally given little direct support to the arts. This was in contrast with its substantial subsidies, support, and protection of business and the national economy.

In 1951, a Royal Commission on National Development in the Arts, Letters and Sciences issued its report. The Commission for the establishment of a Canada Council to give financial support to the arts and sciences, as well as a system of federal scholarships to universities. While a version of the scholarship system was established within a year or two, the idea of the federal government giving, as Prime Minister St. Laurent remarked with distaste, "...money to ballet dancers" fell by the wayside. Even the creation of the national television network was seen by the government as more for the development of the electronics industry than for its cultural and entertainment value.

But slowly, a ground swell of support grew with the founding of two professional ballet organizations and the establishment of the Stratford

Shakespearean Festival in 1953. By 1957, the death of two heirless multi-millionaires gave the government a windfall, with which it then established the Canada Council.

9.11   The Gordon Commission

In 1954, a wealthy Toronto accountant and businessman, Walter Gordon, was invited to Ottawa to meet with the Prime Minister. Gordon, a prominent Liberal, had served in government as a civil servant. St. Laurent wanted Gordon to enter politics and became a junior minister, as he was facing the prospect of a number of prominent cabinet ministers retiring. Gordon refused, mainly because he felt he would have little or no influence as a junior minister in a government dominated by C.D. Howe. Gordon wanted very much to influence Canadian economic policy.

Gordon was the most prominent of a growing group of Canadians who were becoming concerned at Canada's political and economic relationship with the United States. He had begun to write on the subject. One of his articles—shown to some people in Ottawa—had called for a Royal Commission on Canada's Economic Prospects. Gordon was asked if he would forgo publication of the article in exchange for the government taking over his idea and appointing such a commission, with Gordon as its chairman. Gordon agreed.

9.11.1   What the Gordon Commission Found

Like the Massey Commission, which had investigated the state of Canada's arts and culture, the Gordon Commission brought together all the data which developed the extent to which the Canadian economy was being penetrated by the United States. American domination was increasing in the new, developing areas of the economy, such as mineral resources, transportation, and energy, while the influence of Britain was rapidly declining.

Between 1945 and 1957, American investment grew from $7 billion to $17 billion. Most of the money was in direct equity investment and represented over 54 percent of the total Canadian economy. This included 70 percent of the capital in the oil and natural gas industry, 52 percent of mining and smelting, and 43 percent of manufacturing. The

Gordon Commission recognized that there was now a continental economy owned and controlled largely by Americans.

C.D. Howe had been opposed to the creation of the Gordon Commission, which he believed was unnecessary. When the report was released, Howe suggested strongly that the document would be ignored by the government. The Liberal government's position was expressed by B.S. Kierstead, a prominent economist, who said that it was "somewhat naive to suppose that in some fashion this investment constituted a menace to Canadian independence."

9.12   The Pipeline Debate

In 1956, C.D. Howe proposed the construction of an all-Canadian gas pipeline across the prairies to central and southern Ontario (to bring Alberta's natural gas to Canada's industrial heartland). Howe believed that the federal government should be constantly priming the economy with large public projects to stave off recession. To him, the project was both admirable—supplying Canadian needs with a Canadian energy source—and necessary. A cheap, secure energy source was vital to an expanding industrial base.

The project became a controversial one. After extended negotiations and feasibility studies, a plan emerged to create a construction and operating company, albeit American controlled. In order to finance the construction over the most difficult terrain, federal government financial assistance would be required. Both the CCF and Conservatives opposed different elements of the project and decided to filibuster the approval in Parliament. The government, however, pushed through the vote. The ensuing debate was an emotional and raucous one. While the government won the debate, it looked old, tired and arrogant in doing so.

For the first time, Canadians could watch the process on television. Clearly, Canadians were concerned, as the rights of Parliament appeared to have been trampled. And the deal seemed to be another sellout to American interests.

9.13   The Suez Crisis

In international events, 1956 was a tumultuous year. Soviet repression of revolution in Hungary took place just as the Suez Crisis erupted.

When the nationalist leader of Egypt, Colonel Nasser, nationalized the Suez Canal, the British and French had reacted furiously. The Americans adopted an ambivalent position, seeming to support the British and French claims to the canal, on the one hand, yet warning against any armed intervention, on the other hand. Canada tried to distance herself from the crisis, and also warned against military intervention.

When the British and French attack on the Suez finally came, Canada more or less broke with Britain and aligned herself with the United States and the other nations who opposed the invasion. Lester Pearson, External Affairs Minister, tabled a resolution calling for a United Nations peacekeeping force to patrol the canal zone when the British and French forces withdrew. This resolution eventually passed and became the precedent for subsequent U.N. peacekeeping activities. The following year, Pearson won the Nobel Peace Prize.

Canada's break with Britain evoked an immediate public reaction among some Canadians close to the British heritage. Prime Minister St. Laurent, now approaching 75, lost his temper in Parliament, declaring "that the days of the European superman were over."

9.14 "Dief the Chief"

The first victim of the tumultuous political year was, surprisingly, the Leader of the Opposition, George Drew. Drew had already lost two elections to Louis St. Laurent. Drew had led the fight on the pipeline but had often been upstaged by the emotional rhetoric of one of his more prominent colleagues, John Diefenbaker. In any event, Drew became ill and had to resign as leader of the Progressive Conservative Party.

9.14.1 John Diefenbaker

After many attempts, John Diefenbaker had been elected to the House of Commons in 1940. He was already a veteran of the Conservative Party, and a distinguished lawyer. He ran for leadership and lost against John Bracken and George Drew. Finally, when his time came in 1956, the Progressive Conservative Party was enjoying a political revival in the Maritimes and growth of sorts in federal politics because of its spirited campaign in Parliament over the pipeline and its defense of Great Britain during the Suez crisis.

Nevertheless, the party's leadership aspirants appeared to be somewhat mediocre. Diefenbaker, the obvious choice, was distrusted by the party establishment because of his populist independence (especially on social issues, where he often broke with his party).

Diefenbaker was also curiously insensitive to Quebec. At the leadership convention he sparked a temporary walkout by the Quebec delegation because of his refusal to have a Quebecker second his nomination. Instead of being nominated by someone from English and French Canada, he chose to reject, what he called, hyphenated-Canadians, and instead was nominated by a delegate from the Pacific and Atlantic coasts. It was a minor incident in the context of the period but such blindness to Quebec would cost him dearly.

9.14.2 The 1957 Federal Election

If the Liberals were going to fight another election with Louis St. Laurent as leader, they would probably have to go soon. The last year had been particularly difficult on him, and the pressures had brought forth a side of the leader hitherto mostly unseen: he was morose, given to long periods of passive detachment, and he had a short and bitter temper. However, John Diefenbaker was seen by the Liberals as a particularly weak, out of touch, and irrelevant leader. With their base in Quebec unassailable, the problems with the prairie wheat economy and a recent dispute with the Ontario government did not seem to be serious.

One Liberal strategist stated that they would have run with St. Laurent even "if we had to stuff him." And, as they slowly developed a campaign which had no issues—except the government's record and demonstrated competence—St. Laurent often appeared uninspired. Meanwhile, John Diefenbaker, the underdog campaigned furiously across the country. The Liberal campaign slowly fell apart. Yet the final result on June 10, 1957 was a surprise. The Liberals were defeated and John Diefenbaker and the Progressive Conservative Party won a minority government.

Another result of the election, largely unnoticed at the time, was the relatively few seats (25) won by the CCF. The party which was supposed to be the alternative to the Liberals was in fact not.

9.14.3 Lester Bowles Pearson

Louis St. Laurent resigned as leader of the Liberal Party shortly after the June defeat. Lester Pearson was the obvious successor (the party had developed an informal rule by which the leadership alternated between French and English Canadians).

Pearson was one of Canada's first diplomats. He had served in both London and Washington, and had attended most of the important international conferences in which Canada had participated. Pearson was an undersecretary when Louis St. Laurent was a minister. When St. Laurent succeeded Mackenzie-King as Prime Minister, Pearson had moved from the civil service into politics to become the Minister of External Affairs. He was thus one of Canada's most senior and prominent government ministers, yet for most of his life and career he had not been a politician. This disengagement helped him at first in that he did not have to carry the "baggage" of the old government. As Leader of the Opposition with a sterling international record, he had many advantages. (It was announced, the day Parliament under John Diefenbaker resumed, that Pearson was to receive the Nobel Prize.) His political inexperience was to prove shortly to be a huge disadvantage: John Diefenbaker was able to dominate completely in the House, and was able largely to ignore Pearson in the following election.

9.14.4 The Federal Election of 1958

In Parliament, John Diefenbaker's minority government quickly reversed the previous Liberal government's policy of fiscal restraint. Diefenbaker cut taxes, and raised old age pensions. He also advanced grain payments to prairie farmers, who were just beginning to feel the effects of a tightening international grain market.

Nevertheless, the key to the election campaign of 1958 was Diefenbaker's relentless campaign for a new vision of Canada—breaking subordinate ties with the United States while renewing ties with the British Empire, (including a change in trade patterns away from the United States). He also took up cause with—by now, more numerous—nationalist issues. He reached into the "pool" of anti-Americanism which is a constant, if not muted, political instinct in Canada. But more importantly, he proposed an accelerated development program for the north and west and the Maritimes. He won a massive victory—winning

209 seats, including 50 in Quebec. The CCF's share was reduced to a mere eight seats. With only nine percent of the popular vote, the CCF was back to where it began in 1935 when it was founded.

CHAPTER 10

The Conservatives in Power

10.1 Electoral Victory

Instead of losing two consecutive elections, Lester Pearson liked to say that the Liberals had lost one election in two stages. There is some validity to his point. When John Diefenbaker had ended Liberal rule in 1957, he had ended the longest serving, most stable political regime in the country's history. But he did not replace it with a Conservative federal dynasty; instead, the 1957 election ushered in the most tumultuous political decade Canada has ever had. In the following ten years, there would be five general elections, two changes of governments, and four minority governments.

10.2 The Economy

A relatively minor economic slump emerged in 1957. The slump was caused mainly by a fall in foreign investment, due to worldwide economic problems. There was little the Diefenbaker government could do. It did launch an aggressive campaign to expand and to diversify Canadian foreign trade; but except for some agricultural markets, most foreign objectives were unmet. Diefenbaker's election promise to divert trade to Great Britain was largely unmet. (Indeed, Britain was making overtures to join the European Common Market, which would mean a further shifting of British trade away from Canada and an end to the Commonwealth trade preferences.)

Despite all the rhetoric and efforts to move away from American economic control, Canada in fact became a closer economic partner of the United States.

10.2.1 Chinese Wheat Sales

Canadian wheat sales abroad were declining—and prices were falling—when Diefenbaker took office. This coincided with two poor harvests in a row. The government, with some of its strongest ministers representing the West, moved quickly to short up the Western farm economy with a number of programs and subsidies. They also began an aggressive export campaign, including a large sale to China in 1960.

The Chinese wheat sale in particular (sales were also made to the USSR) annoyed the American government. However, despite American protests, the Canadian government went ahead with the sales and the prairie economy thrived. Farm income nearly tripled.

10.2.2 The Avro Arrow and the Bomarc

Through the 1950s, Canada had been developing jet aircraft. It began as work on a passenger model and then a switch was made to a pure jet fighter plane. In the context of the times, this move seemed logical. The perceived Soviet threat to the North American continent had forced a closer bilateral relationship between Canada and the United States. Cooperation on the development of radar warning lines in the Canadian north lead to an agreement on joint North American Air Defense, which was signed in 1957.

Work on the Arrow (the CF105) proved more costly than expected. By the time a prototype was developed, the United States had already signalled its decision not to purchase the plane. Diefenbaker moved to halt production of the Arrow in early 1959. Amid bitter outcries, 14 000 engineers, scientists, and skilled workers were jobless.

Diefenbaker justified his decision cancelling the Arrow slightly illogically, on the grounds that the day of the manned bomber was over, and that he would purchase the U.S. Bomarc missile as well as the almost obsolete American fighter aircraft to act as backup. The Bomarc was effective only against bomber attack (it had never really been tested properly), and was useless without an atomic warhead.

Even though Canada was a pioneer in atomic research, and the leading producer of uranium, it had voluntarily renounced nuclear weapons. Canada's Minister of External Affairs, Howard Green, wanted Canada to shift away from the United States and become essentially non-aligned. He was adamantly opposed to nuclear proliferation. While the government was split on the issue, a large and vocal peace movement was growing in Canada. Diefenbaker was torn. The issue came to a head in 1962 when the Bomarcs were installed.

10.3   The New Democratic Party

The Conservative victory in 1958 was a shattering blow to the CCF. Not only had the party failed to convince the public that it was the alternative to the Liberals, its own supporters had deserted it at the polls.

The issue now was to modernize and modify its relatively extreme socialist program, to call instead for social reforms and full employment policies. By this means, the party hoped to forge a coalition between the rural cooperative movement—which had always been its traditional source of strength—and the growing trade union movement in the industrial provinces, which seemed also to be moving to the CCF.

With the formal support and affiliation of the Canadian Labour Congress, the New Democratic Party (NDP) was formed.

CHAPTER 11

Renewed Unrest

11.1 The Political Climate of 1963

Author Peter C. Newman once described the ship of state under John Diefenbaker as "the Titanic…an inevitable rush to disaster…sinking at the end in a galaxy of fireworks, brass bands playing and the captain shouting hysterical orders to crewmen who had long since jumped overboard."

11.1.1 The Fall in 1963

John Diefenbaker's minority government may have gained time to consolidate itself had he tried to broker the divided House of Commons, but he seemed incapable of doing so. He also seemed incapable of deciding whether or not to accept nuclear warheads for the Bomarc. In January 1963, Lester Pearson suddenly reversed the Liberal position and announced that since Canada had committed itself to accepting nuclear weapons, it should live up to that commitment. The White House had openly assisted the Liberals in the previous campaign; now the State Department directly challenged Prime Minister Diefenbaker with a blunt statement that Canada had made no proposal "sufficiently practical to contribute effectively to North American defense." Douglas Harkness, Minister of Defense, resigned. On February 5, 1963, the government resigned as a result of a vote of no-confidence. This was a first in Canadian history.

11.1.2 Federal Election of 1963

The resignation of Douglas Harkness opened a leadership split in the Conservative Party. As Diefenbaker took to the campaign trail, he did so deserted by a large part of his cabinet and with the rank and file of the party confused and discouraged by the events of the past two years. However, if John Diefenbaker could not govern, he certainly could campaign. Although he was Prime Minister, he campaigned as the underdog, claiming that all the powers of the establishment— including the popular American president, John F. Kennedy—were ranged against him. His appeal to the latent anti-American, nationalist feeling in the country was effective, but not effective enough. This time it was a Liberal government. The Conservatives managed to retain 95 seats.

Diefenbaker was able to keep his Western—mainly rural—base. In Quebec, however, the Conservative share of the popular vote dropped from 50 percent in 1958 to less than 19 percent in 1963. Rural Quebec, while rejecting the Conservatives, again did not return to the Liberals. Instead, it stayed with the Social Credit (Crediteste) Party.

11.2 The New Quebec

The longtime premier of Quebec, Maurice Duplessis, ruled the province like a feudal estate. He controlled the press, the courts, even the church (which, in turn, controlled the educational system). By appealing to the national conscience of the people, Duplessis was able to dominate Quebec (which was changing and industrializing at almost the same pace as the rest of Canada). He was able to project himself as the protector of the French culture, language, and heritage against the encroachments of the "Anglos" in the form of the federal government. But when he died suddenly in 1959, his political machine collapsed.

In the provincial election in 1960, the Liberal Party, led by Jean Lesage, formed the government. It was a government pledged to end the corruption of the Duplessis years, but more important to modernize Quebec in every sense of the word. Most historians consider the election of the Liberals in 1960 as the beginning of *"The Quiet Revolution."*

Perhaps the most important act of the first Lesage government was to create Quebec Hydro out of the tangled network of private utilities in the province. This nationalization under the slogan of "Masters in our own House" brought another election, in which the Union Nationale—Duplessis's old party—was virtually wiped out. Other reforms now followed, the most important being the removal of the church from the public educational system. In 1964, the first Quebec Department of Education was established.

11.2.1 Federal/Provincial Relations

Throughout the war and post-war periods, the essential conflict between the provinces and the federal government had been over finances (taxation) and jurisdiction over new areas of expanded government action. Both levels of government needed more money. This tension between provincial and federal authorities was perhaps normal, and typical of all modernizing states. In Canada, these pressures were exacerbated by the confusing interpretation of powers within the BNA Act, and the existence of stated and unstated distinctions between Quebec and the other provinces.

These problems prevented Canada from patriating its constitution from the British Parliament, because no amending formula could be found to address these concerns. While various constitutional proposals had been advanced since the issue was first raised in 1927, no real progress was made. For the most part, then, federal/provincial discussions centred upon tax sharing agreements and measures that would allow federal/provincial cooperation in overlapping and disputed jurisdictions. Cost-sharing programs could work if both levels of government had similar priorities and goals. This was clearly not the case in Canada, where the goal of Quebec society was, at the least, to maintain autonomy.

While Quebec modernized, the country as a whole increasingly had a new social agenda requiring an activist federal government. The question became one of cooperative federalism, and could no longer be finessed by various tax and cost-sharing schemes.

Inspired in part by the U.S. civil rights movement and the anti-colonial movement in Asia and Africa, a separatist movement developed in Quebec. Slogans such as "A hundred years of injustice" and books—one entitled *The White Niggers of America*—gained currency. Thus, while the renewal and democratization of Quebec society made Quebec more like the rest of Canada, the separatist movement gained strength.

John Diefenbaker, on the one hand, was blind to this phenomenon. He established simultaneous translation in the House of Commons, and a bilingual federal government, thinking this was sufficient. In opposition he became a "lightning rod" for anti-French sentiment throughout Canada. Lester Pearson, on the other hand, felt the pressures from Quebec; and while he did not advance any constitutional solutions, he did attempt to address some long-standing grievances. He also established what was to become the most important study of the ethnic, cultural, and social makeup of Canada, The Royal Commission on Bilingualism and Biculturalism. However, by the time the Commission's final reports were ready, Pearson's successor, Pierre Elliot Trudeau, was in office with firm ideas of his own.

11.2.2 Sixty Days of Decision

As the election campaign of 1963 developed, the anxious Liberals saw their advantages fall away as John Diefenbaker waged his courageous, virtually single-handed struggle. Finally, drawing on the Liberal reputation for smooth, effective administration, Lester Pearson announced "Sixty Days of Decision" in which a new Liberal government would, among other sweeping reforms, bring in a federal budget. The context for this promise was not only Diefenbaker's effective campaign, but also the fact that the Canadian dollar was falling.

Walter Gordon, a close personal and political friend of Pearson and leader of the party's nationalist wing, was Minister of Finance. Within the 60 days, he produced a budget. The mildly expansionist budget contained some nationalist rhetoric proposing a surtax on any foreign ("American") takeover of any existing Canadian company. The ensuing protest forced a budget revision. An embarrassed Pearson finally had to disown his finance minister.

11.2.3 Pearson and Kennedy

The Pearson government moved immediately to accept nuclear weapons for the Bomarc and for Canada's NATO fighter planes. Pearson visited Kennedy, renewing a long-standing personal friendship and discussing a whole range of bilateral issues, including Canada's now serious trade deficit with the United States and balance of payments problem.

11.2.4 The Auto Pact

The main source of Canada's balance of payments problem lay within the auto industry. This industry—although almost wholly American owned—was oriented to the Canadian domestic market and to exports to the British Commonwealth. With the Commonwealth market largely defunct, the Canadian industry was too large and specialized for domestic consumption. The solution was to integrate the North American industry. Canada thus negotiated an auto trade agreement with the United States. In this agreement, provisions were made to protect production in Canada. While Canada abandoned any pretence of a independent automobile industry, it solved—almost with one stroke—Canada's balance of payments crisis and gave a measure of security to the auto industry. The industry remains the economic manufacturing base of Ontario.

11.2.5 Economic Relations

Within a week of the withdrawal of Walter Gordon's surtax on foreign investment in Canada, the United States moved to stem a serious outflow of U.S. capital abroad. The government announced its own surtax on American capital flowing abroad. Ironically, Walter Gordon—instead of being pleased that the American government was doing what he wanted his own tax to do—rushed to the United States to plead for an exemption for Canada from this new regulation. At first, the United States resisted, arguing that Canada was one of the main borrowers of American capital. Whatever the reasons, Canada was given an exemption but in return Canada had to give the United States virtual veto power over Canadian monetary policy.

11.2.6 Federal Election of 1965

By 1965, the Liberal government had a number of achievements. Although the same rapport that had existed between Lester Pearson and John F. Kennedy was not re-established with Lyndon Johnson, both governments shared a sense of social activism. In Canada, the economy stabilized; and with the Auto Pact and the Columbia River project now complete, relations with the U.S. were warm and productive. If the war in Vietnam was beginning to cast a shadow over this relationship, it was offset by Canada's preventative action, averting a major crisis in NATO by sending troops to separate Greeks and Turks on Cyrpus, and by the domestic economic advantages to Canada of being a supplier to the growing U.S. war effort.

Domestically, the opposition was split. The Conservative Party was preoccupied in trying to find ways to displace John Diefenbaker. Also, the Social Credit Party had split into two wings.

The government had fought a bruising battle, but had nevertheless been successful in adopting a distinctive Canadian flag in 1964. It had developed a new contributory pension plan (the Canada Pension Plan) and had set the wheels in motion for a national medicare program.

The Royal Commission on Bilingualism and Biculturalism had issued its first report, highlighting the seriousness of the constitutional issue yet implying as well that solutions could be found.

With all this activity, Lester Pearson's advisors convinced him to call an election to try to secure a majority government.

The election result saw little change in the composition of Parliament. There would still be a minority Liberal government. This would be the last election for Pearson, and Diefenbaker would shortly be removed as leader of the Conservatives. The NDP or New Democratic Party took some comfort in that it received 19 percent of the vote, including some support in Quebec. Perhaps the most significant outcome of the election was the emergence of a new Quebec presence on the federal scene, in the form of what was dubbed "The Three Wise Men": Jean Marchand, a well known trade union leader; Gerard Pelletier, a prominent journalist, and sometime law professor; and Pierre Trudeau, journalist, civil rights lawyer, and peace movement activist. All three had been recruited by the Liberals for the 1965 election.

11.2.7 Everything Changes: Everything Remains the Same

The sole issue as far as the ruling Liberals were concerned in the 1965 election was the need for a majority government. This was not achieved, and things went on very much as before. The Canada Pension Plan was implemented before the election. But the compromise—which allowed Quebec keep the monies raised by the premiums within the province—would not be as easy to reach when the next issue, medicare, came on to the agenda. The nationalist movement in Quebec, moreover, had grown. Premier Lesage now demanded Quebec's right to negotiate international agreements in areas such as education—where Quebec had jurisdiction. While it was one thing to argue over tax-sharing and revenue issues, it was quite another to raise issues of autonomy to the level of international negotiations.

Nationalist and separatist pressures continued to grow in Quebec. The Liberal government of Jean Lesage had been defeated in a provincial election; and the new premier of a revitalized Union Nationale made even greater demands and put more strains on Quebec's fragile relationship in Canada. Then, in the midst of Canada's Centennial celebrations, the President of France, Charles DeGaulle, made a triumphant tour from Quebec City up the St. Lawrence Valley to Montreal. He compared his tour to his return to France near the end of World War II. From the balcony of Montreal's City Hall, he shouted out the slogan of the separatists: "Vive Le Quebec Libre". An outraged Lester Pearson announced that neither Quebec nor Canada needed liberation. DeGaulle returned home, but the issue was now in the open: the country was split.

Even though the relationship with the United States remained correct and at times cordial, the easy rapport between Kennedy and Pearson did not long outlast the former's death. Canada, and Lester Pearson, always viewed American activities in Cuba, and Latin America in general, with great suspicion. Pearson was known to have opposed French and American involvement in South-East Asia, although he was sympathetic with American aims. Pearson did raise his misgivings with Kennedy, and until the end of the war did nothing to stop or even hinder the American war effort.

But public pressure against the war grew in Canada, as it did in the U.S. There were a number of "pressure points." The Canadian government did nothing to stop American draft dodgers or deserters from immigrating into Canada. Canadians often greeted these young men quite warmly. This annoyed the U.S. government, but by and large, nothing really disturbed the relationship. The Canadian government resisted increasing public pressure to distance the country from the war by maintaining a policy it described as "quiet diplomacy." This posture was maintained until 1965, when Lester Pearson spoke at an American university and called for a bombing halt. This infuriated Lyndon Johnson, and Pearson later privately apologized. But relations remained cool.

11.2.8 Rene Levesque

Rene Levesque was a prominent journalist and television personality before he entered politics. He was first elected to the Quebec Assembly in 1960 with the Lesage government, and quickly became one of its most prominent ministers. It was Levesque who masterminded the creation of Quebec Hydro. This rapidly became the symbol of the new Quebec and dominated the re-election campaign as an example of the slogan "Masters in Our Own House."

Always a nationalist, Levesque quickly gave up on notions of "cooperative federalism." In his mind, Quebec had its own social, economic, and political agenda, and this agenda was being stifled by the political domination of English Canada in the form of a strong federal government. Levesque wanted a new relationship, which he was later to describe as "sovereignty-association."

As a private citizen, Levesque published *Opinion Quebec* in September 1967. This manifesto seemed to be a clear demand for independence. When the Liberal Party rejected it, Levesque walked out and on November 18, 1967, he founded the *Mouvement souverainete-association.*

The long arguments about "what does Quebec want?" could now come to an end. What had hitherto been a fringe movement of the political right and left, was now approaching mainstream politics with a recognized leader and a clear set of political objectives.

11.2.9 Pierre Elliot Trudeau

The least likely of the "three wise men" in the 1965 election was Pierre Trudeau. Not only was he not a Liberal, but he had also waged a vigorous public campaign against their nuclear policy. At one point, he called Lester Pearson "the defrocked prince of peace."

As a political activist, Trudeau was associated with many left-wing causes. Indeed, in 1963 he was the campaign manager for the NDP candidate in the constituency he would successfully contest for the Liberals two years later.

However, Trudeau's entrance into Federal politics as a Liberal was a mark of his political consistency. While Trudeau was active in the labour and civil rights movements, he was consistently opposed to nationalism of any sort. He quickly lost sympathy with his friend Rene

Levesque as the latter's nationalism became more pronounced. Once elected, Trudeau quickly distinguished himself as a constitutional affairs advisor to Lester Pearson. Within a year, he was appointed Minister of Justice. In that portfolio he became well-known and extremely popular, as he reformed Canada's archaic divorce laws and liberalized and modernized the criminal code. He became famous for the quip that, "the state has no business in the bedrooms of the nation."

Like Pearson, Trudeau was a strong federalist. Unlike Pearson and many other federalists, Trudeau had a very clear idea of the separation of powers between federal and provincial interests, and he was unprepared to accept any notions of "special status" for Quebec. He strongly opposed any devolution of federal powers among any or all of the provinces. He combined this strong federalist position with an equally strong determination that the federal system must provide equal opportunities for all Canadians. He would tell Quebeckers to be masters of their own house, but that they should consider all of Canada to be their house.

11.2.10 The Conservative Party in Opposition

Robert Stanfield has often been described as the best Prime Minister Canada never had. After several years of divisions, splits, and plots, the Progressive Conservative Party finally replaced John Diefenbaker as leader with the then premier of Nova Scotia, Robert Stanfield.

It was obvious to most observers after the federal election of 1967 that neither John Diefenbaker nor Lester Pearson would ever gain the full confidence of the Canadian people.

After Diefenbaker's defeat in 1962, a conservative professor, George Grant, wrote a book entitled *Lament for a Nation* in which he described the defeat as a crucial turning point in Canadian history, meaning the virtual end of Canada. It was an impressive argument, portraying Diefenbaker as the last best hope for the country. But Diefenbaker's anti-Americanism was based on nostalgic harking back for an empire and colony that no longer was. Diefenbaker was, by now, largely irrelevant. Now relegated to the Opposition, Diefenbaker led an increasingly divided caucus on continual tirade against everything that could be considered anti-British or anything that could be considered downgrading the Crown. Diefenbaker had long held the belief that the only thing which stood in the way of Canada's absorption into the

United States was the British Crown. This preoccupation of his reached its peak as he brought the country literally to a halt in a debate over a distinctive Canadian flag.

Diefenbaker's appeal had a certain resonance among sections of Canada. The old British colonial symbols—which Diefenbaker valued—may have been respected by sections of English Canada, but they were increasingly alien to new generations of Canadians who traced their backgrounds to other countries. These symbols were also offensive to new generations of Quebeckers.

As the Conservative Party hewed to Diefenbaker's line, it became more isolated in Quebec and threatened to become marginalized in the rest of urban Canada. The dilemma for the Conservatives increased as it became obvious that Canadians were unhappy with the current Liberal government. A new leader and a new policy would change everything.

As was the case before, first came the new policy then the new leader. A Conservative Thinkers Conference was held in Montmorency Quebec in early 1967. A new speaker for Quebec came forward, a successful businessman, Marcel Fairibault, announcing that Canada had to be described as consisting of "two nations" and that the country should work from there to frame a new constitution.

A few months later, Robert Stanfield was elected leader of the party with a mandate to build enough strength in Quebec to form a new national consensus and, more importantly, a new federal government.

Meanwhile the Liberals had a better idea.

CHAPTER 12

Prime Minister Trudeau

12.1 The Federal Election of 1968

Pierre Trudeau captured the Liberal leadership by a margin of three votes on the fourth ballot. Trudeau's popularity rested with the public at large. Riding a wave of what was termed "Trudeaumania," he confidently promised to continue with the Liberal tradition of social legislation—building what he described as a "just society". But it was on the constitutional issue—where he bluntly called for a strong federal government, with no special status or concessions to Quebec—where his appeal resonated in English Canada. Paradoxically, he maintained a strong Liberal following in Quebec, with his appeal for "French Power" in Ottawa and all federal institutions. The result, largely a forgone conclusion, was the first majority government in a decade. In Quebec, the Liberals won 56 out of a possible 74 seats.

12.2 The October Crisis

Since the early 1960s, Quebec had been the scene of several, mostly minor, terrorist incidents. Statues and other symbolic artifacts were the usual targets of clandestine groups such as the FLQ (Front de Liberation du Quebec). In one case, a watchman at an army recruiting depot was killed by a bomb explosion.

On the morning of October 5, 1970, James Cross, senior British Trade Representative in Montreal, was kidnapped by members of the FLQ. Demands were issued for the release of "political prisoners", reading of the *Manifesto of the FLQ* over the radio, and some other concessions. Trudeau and the young and recently elected Premier of Quebec, Robert Bourassa, began negotiations. After the manifesto was read over the air, the Quebec government announced that no prisoners would be released. Pierre Laporte, Minister of Labor was then kidnapped from his home. Negotiations continued in an increasingly confused public atmosphere. Student demonstrations took place, and at one point several prominent Quebec figures urged more serious negotiations and concessions. Trudeau refused.

The federal government proclaimed the War Measures Act. Declaring an "apprehended insurrection," the army was put on the streets and civil liberties suspended. The FLQ was declared illegal. Several hundred arrests were made. Two days later, the body of Pierre Laporte was found.

In November, arrests were made in the Laporte case, and a month later, James Cross was found unharmed.

In English Canada, Trudeau's decisive action was well received. Yet as time passed, very few charges were ever laid against the detainees and the FLQ was shown to be a mere handful of people. In short, there really had been no insurrection.

12.3 The Just Society

The 1960s in Canada, as in most Western nations, were marked by social protest and reform. A number of reform initiatives by the previous activist government came to fruition during the first Trudeau administration, whereas others came to a sudden halt. A report on Canada's tax structure, which proposed to develop a more equitable and simpler tax regime, was dropped. An early effort to find a way to finance gradual absorption of the aboriginal population into the mainstream of society—to end their isolation and poverty—also floundered.

Trudeau ordered studies on Canada's defense and foreign policies. Both studies were an attempt to move the country away from its vision of itself as an international helpful "fixer," to one which attempting more to serve Canada's economic interests and concerns. While overtures were made to China, the Soviet Union, and relations with Cuba were strengthened, it was hard, in the context of the Cold War, to determine what were Canada's interests and where they lay.

In defense matters, Trudeau had long been skeptical of a Soviet military menace; having Canadian troops defend Europe while having virtually none at home seemed wasteful. Some troops were withdrawn from NATO, and the Canadian commitment reduced. But for the most part, Trudeau bowed to pressure and kept Canadian bases open in Germany. The Canadian military was cut, however. The Canadian forces, recently reorganized, were combined and geared to a expanded role as peacekeepers.

12.4   The Victoria Charter

As the demands of Quebec increased to what Quebec Premier Daniel Johnson called "Associates Statehood" in the mid-1960s, other provinces, notably Ontario, demanded more powers. The smaller, weaker, and poorer provinces wanted a larger federal presence, more assistance, and more equalization payments. The federal government was torn between these conflicting demands and its own insistance on a strong federal or central authority.

To meet these competing demands, the federal government embarked on several cost-sharing programs, such as medicare and the Canada Pension Plan. It also broadened the range and concept of federal programs such as Unemployment Insurance.

In 1969, the federal government organized the *Department of Regional Economic Expansion* whose mandate was to revitalize the economy of the economically depressed areas. By 1972, it was pumping almost $600 million annually into the Maritime economy.

In less direct economic terms, an image of a strong federal presence was at the heart of the *Official Languages Act of 1969*, which gave French and English equal status in the eyes of the federal government. This was reinforced by efforts to make Canadian society bilingual.

These federal efforts form the background for stepped up efforts to create a constitution that would reflect the country's true nature and provide for a division of powers that would somehow balance regionalism with centralization. In 1971, these discussions reached a climax of sorts in Victoria, British Columbia, where the federal government and all the provincial premiers agreed to the *Victoria Charter*. This charter was a series of federal/provincial tradeoffs. Most of the concrete demands were put off for later discussions, but the main tradeoff was an agreement that Ontario and Quebec would have veto rights over any future constitutional change. Although he agreed to the Charter in Victoria, Bourassa then quickly rejected to compromise because public opinion saw Quebec's future aspirations frozen by the Charter. For a few years, constitution-making would again be a dead issue.

12.5 Economic Concerns

The economy—which, in the later 1960s, was driven largely by increasing demands of the U.S. war economy—began to falter. This was a spillover from the United States, and there seemed little that Canada could do. The unemployment rate was rising, but more urgent was the rising inflation rate. The term "stagflation" came into wide currency, and the Keynesian model, which had been at the core of economic thinking since the Great Depression, came under new scrutiny.

Canada's economy did not share the American balance of payments problem, which, by 1970, was becoming a crisis. Indeed, as America's largest trading partner—there is more trade between the United States and Ontario than with the United States and Japan—Canada could be seen as part of the U.S. problem.

In August 1971, President Richard Nixon announced a wide-ranging set of tax incentives and tax credits designed to repatriate American investments abroad and to discourage further capital exports. The regulations also served to restrict multinational imports from their own foreign plants and encourage exports. Nixon bluntly refused to exempt Canada.

This came as a tremendous shock to Canada, and while some listless attempts were made to explore a "third option" of increased European trade—there was not much Canada could do. Canada tried to convince the Americans to reconsider or to make other adjustments, but Nixon, soon to be consumed with other problems, did not discuss the issue.

That is about where matters stood with the Canadian economy with the 1972 election campaign looming.

12.6 The Federal Election of 1972

In retrospect, one can see that the "Nixon shock" was the signal that easy days for Canada's economy were over. Even so, the government could be excused for thinking that the economic decline was a temporary blip—Iranian oil was still selling for U.S. 50 cents a barrel, and even Western agriculture would overcome recent poor crops. With the bland slogan, "The Land is Strong" Trudeau announced the 1972 election and refused to campaign. He would have a leisurely dialogue with the people. Meanwhile the other political parties campaigned earnestly, with the result that the election was the closest in Canadian history—109 Liberals elected compared to 107 Conservatives. If Trudeau was going to continue in office he would need help.

12.7   Minority Government

Most political observers credit Pierre Trudeau's near defeat with his government's insensitivity to Canada's economic problems and to individual Canadians. Government mismanagement or disinterest was also apparent.

Trudeau had to govern during the next period with the support of the leftist, and nationalist, New Democratic Party. To maintain their support he created Petro-Canada, a government oil company, which would become one of the major players in the industry. He would try to win back a measure of Canadian control over the energy sector. He created a Foreign Investment Review Agency to oversee foreign take-overs, and to accept them only if they met certain criteria. A Canadian Development Corporation was also organized to provide an industrial policy, including government investment and ownership.

The government also announced new social security measures, unemployment insurance was expanded again, family allowances and pensions were increased and indexed to the cost of living. Income tax exemptions were also linked to the rate of inflation.

Although the economic situation did not improve greatly, Liberal popularity increased enough that, by 1974, the government was ready to call another election.

12.7.1   Quebec and Canada

The failure of the *Victoria Charter* ended formal constitutional negotiations for a decade. However, the issue of Quebec/Canada relations increased in intensity.

The revival of the Union Nationale did not outlive Premier Daniel Johnson, who died suddenly in 1970. With the defeat of the Union Nationale by a revitalized Liberal Party led by a young economist, Robert Bourassa, the "Quiet Revolution" seemed to enter a new phase. Quebec was overburdened with debt and its relatively small industrial base, concentrated in textile, furniture, shoes, etc. was increasingly fragile. Bourassa dismissed the nationalist gestures and symbols and called for a "profitable confederation". He promised a modern techno-cratic and efficient government. Above all, he promised jobs.

The Liberals won the election in 1970 and were re-elected in 1972. Journalists and political pundits declared separatism dead. What was overlooked, however, was the fact that Rene Levesque had been able to weld a highly fractious coalition into a viable political party that was both separatist and social-democratic. In the provincial election of 1970, the Parti Quebecois won just a fifth of the vote. But it was the only alternative in what was now, with the Union Nationale defunct, a two party state.

12.7.2 Multiculturalism

The complex question of Canada's multicultural character arose with increasing intensity as English/French divisions forced political scientists and others to reassess the country's nature. More than a third of Canada, in fact, was neither French nor Anglo-Saxon. And if the majority of other immigrants—and now their children and grandchil-dren—were formerly from central and western Europe, the most recent immigrants have been called "visible minorities"—people of color from Asia, Africa, and Latin America.

In this vein, a biographer of Pierre Trudeau, Richard Gwyn, has written: "So Trudeau had been criticized for ignoring the Queen: in 1973 the Queen came to Canada twice…with Trudeau at her side every step of the royal progress. So he had been accused of sloughing off the ethnics: up sprang a trebled multicultural program that functioned as a slush fund to buy ethnic votes."

There is more an element of historical truth and logic in Gwyn's cynical criticism of multiculturalism. The separatist leader Rene Levesque called the whole issue a "red Herring…devised to obscure the 'Quebec business….'" Even so, Canada is a nation of immigrants not unlike the United States. But because of its late development, the binational character of its founding, and its colonial status, an approach akin to the 19th century U.S. "melting pot" was never acceptable or even possible in Canada. Instead, the idea of a "cultural mosaic" developed in Canada, which was finally codified in 1971 as *The Act for the Preservation and Enhancement of Multiculturalism in Canada*. From this act flowed a number of entitlements which now characterize the country.

12.7.3 Federal Election of 1974

With new attention and resolve to solve economic and social problems, the government decided once more to go to the people. Under Robert Stanfield, the Progressive Conservative's campaigned earnestly, and, in what many consider to be a serious blunder, a positive manner. The government was not solving many of the underlying economic and social problems, and seemed instead merely to be throwing money at issues. World oil prices were rising and the inflation rate was now hitting 10 percent. Wages were also rising, nonetheless, the Conservatives called for wage and price controls: the Liberals ridiculed them.

The Liberals were returned to power with a majority government while weakened in the West, but they held urban Ontario, and, more importantly, they held 60 out of 74 Quebec constituencies, garnering 54 percent of the popular vote.

12.8 The New Majority

The Liberals fought the 1974 election campaign on the promise that whatever Canada's economic problems were, they were neither drastic, nor did they require sweeping government intervention. Oil prices had risen, but Canada was virtually energy self-sufficient; and any temporary economic dislocation could be cushioned by a government-supported price well below the world price.

However, the price of oil continued to rise, and resentment grew in the oil-producing provinces over oil sales at relatively low prices as did the costs to the federal government of keeping prices below world price.

Unemployment continued to rise as did inflation. The federal government began to incur growing deficits as it made different attempts to stimulate the economy and to control costs.

12.8.1 Wage and Price Controls

Finally, within a year of winning the election on the promise not to impose wage and price controls, the government reversed its position. A system of wage and price controls—with the concurrent establishment of monitoring agencies—was announced suddenly. Wage increases were to be capped and some workers who settled contracts before the retroactive deadline were exempt while others were not. Over the next three years, wage increases were to be reduced to six percent annually by 1977. Prices were also to be monitored, although they were almost impossible to control. At the end of the three year period, wages were effectively controlled. But it can be argued whether it was the controls or the general economic climate which moderated pay demands. The general rate of inflation hardly changed.

The political damage to Pierre Trudeau and his government was enormous. The notion that he was untrustworthy was current; but perhaps even more damaging was the growing feeling that his government was incompetent and incapable of managing the economy.

12.8.2 Federal/Provincial Relations

Long-held regional grievances—particularly in the West—that the federal government was concerned only with Ontario and Quebec gained force with the oil price spiral.

The producing provinces wanted to sell their oil at world prices, and they wanted to keep a larger share of royalties. The federal government—with the backing of Ontario mainly—wanted a national price, a greater share of the royalties, and more important, control of the industry. While this issue was fought mainly with the major producing provinces, control over energy was a key concern of Quebec because it was developing the first stage of the James Bay hydro project. Significant oil discoveries were also made off the coast of Newfoundland, a "have-not" province, and the issue of control over future resources also became an issue there.

12.8.3 Quebec Language Laws

An important element in Quebec's struggle to preserve its culture and traditions has been the implicit idea of the province as an embattled French enclave or island in a continental "sea" of English. The Royal Commission on Bilingualism and Biculturalism, as well as various census (1971 in particular) reports, found evidence to suggest that French was endangered in Quebec. The policy of allowing parents full choice in the language of instruction for their children had meant that post-war immigrants were assimilating into English culture in Montreal and other urban centres in the province. French Canadians, who had formed over 83 percent of the population of Quebec in the 1950s, were a declining percentage of the population. The issue of French education was building as the economy faltered. Indeed, there was a riot in a Montreal suburb over language of instruction.

The federal Liberals had always stated that the solution to the language issue was to make all of Canada bilingual. English Canada had, for the most part, been sullenly hostile on the issue. However, in 1976, an innocuous regulation allowing bilingual air traffic control in Quebec caused a wave of reaction, including a strike by pilots and controllers—forcing the government to withdraw the plan for further study. The issue was then forgotten in English Canada. When the new study was completed, and bilingual air-traffic control was instituted in Quebec, nobody seemed to notice. But the issue was not forgotten in Quebec. Finally, Premier Bourassa introduced legislation making French the official language in Quebec and restricting access to English education. The legislation outraged the federal Liberals, who were calling for Canada-wide bilingualism, and offended Quebec nationalists who thought the legislation did not go far enough in defending the province's language and culture.

12.8.4 Quebec Election of 1976

Prior to 1976, the Parti Quebecois (P.Q.) had contested two elections. It garnered public support and had become the Official Opposition in the Quebec National Assembly. Its leader, Rene Levesque, was an effective and popular leader. However, the party was a separatist one, and separatism was clearly a minority position (even among the French who made up 80 percent of the province's population).

By 1976, the Bourassa government seemed embattled on all sides. The economy was in tatters and Bourassa had several conflicts with the provincial trade-union movement, at one time jailing some of its leaders. The language issue had split his own party. In an atmosphere of weakness, incompetence, and corruption, he called an election, fully expecting to lose some support but realizing that as the only federalist party, he would probably be re-elected.

The P.Q., instead of campaigning for independence, made "good government" its theme, with a social democratic election platform strongly emphasizing openness and honesty in government. The party won the election. Thus, on November 15, 1976, the first separatist government was elected in Quebec. Although it did not run on a program of independence—"sovereignty association"—such was clearly the raison-d'étre of the party. It promised a referendum on the issue before its mandate had expired.

12.8.5 Joe Clark

In 1976, Joe Clark a young, virtually unknown member of Parliament, was chosen to succeed Progressive Conservative leader Robert Stanfield. Clark, an Albertan, agreed with the Premier of Alberta, Peter Lougheed, on the need for more control over the province's natural resources. He also supported Western demands for a better royalty split on oil prices, the privatization of the government's oil company Petro-Canada, as well as less interventionist government generally. His constitutional position was to devolve federal government powers to the provinces. "Canada," he said, "was a community of communities."

12.8.6 The Federal Election of 1979

The election of 1979 appeared to bring the Trudeau era in Canadian politics to an end. The Liberals tried to win support with calls for strong central government and Trudeau's now passionate preoccupation with returning the constitution from Britain with an amending formula and a Charter of Rights—none of which the provincial premiers to agree to. The Liberals suffered severe losses in the western provinces and even in Ontario. Trudeau, nonetheless, was able to increase his support in Quebec. Such support (114 seats in a 282 seat Parliament), while not sufficient to retain power, was enough to prevent the Conservatives from forming a majority government. Trudeau became Leader of the Opposition for a few listless months, and then announced his resignation.

Joe Clark, at 39, became Canada's youngest Prime Minister. Sensing the Liberal disorganization and weakness, Clark announced that he intended to govern as if he had a majority. That was his first mistake.

12.8.7 Provincial Rights

Clark's emphasis on negotiation and creating regional harmony and equality seemed, at first, a welcome change from Trudeau's confrontational style. But in substantive negotiations with the more powerful premiers, such as Lougheed of Alberta, Clark appeared weak and equivocal. Inflation was still accelerating, and Clark's efforts to meet the demands of the oil-producing provinces could have been interpreted as weakness. Public opinion quickly turned against the young government.

12.8.8 The 1979 Budget

A very "hard-nosed" budget was introduced in Parliament. Clark refused to make any concessions or even make any overtures to the minority parties for support. Perhaps seeking to repeat the Diefenbaker victories of 1967 and 1958, Clark challenged Parliament in a vote of confidence. Overlooking that he was 20 percentage points behind the Liberals in the opinion polls and that even the Conservative premier of Ontario had denounced his budget, Clark was "trapped".

12.8.9 Federal Election of 1980

The Conservatives campaigned on an appeal to "Give Real Change a Fair Chance". The Liberals, leaderless for a few days, finally had Trudeau back but with an even more vague campaign agenda. Ontario, Quebec, and the Maritimes secured for the Liberals a majority government—147 seats to 103 seats. The Creditistes were wiped out, and the NDP won 32 seats. The Conservatives were reduced to one seat in Quebec; and the Liberals held only one seat west of the Great Lakes, in Winnipeg. There was no national party with a national mandate.

CHAPTER 13

"Welcome to the Eighties"

13.1 Trudeau's Vision

On election night February 18, 1980, a victorious Pierre Trudeau spoke to his celebrating supporters, "Welcome to the 1980s". He reaffirmed that his would be his last election, and in this sense, he was free to govern as saw fit. The popular perception, in central Canada at least, was that he could handle the rebellious West just as he could handle the Quebec separatists. What he could or would do about the economy, with both inflation and unemployment rising, was another question.

13.1.1 The Quebec Referendum

The P.Q. had promised to hold a referendum in Quebec on sovereignty-association during its first mandate. Time was now running out. Faced with the knowledge that the majority of Quebeckers did not want separation, the Quebec government prepared a cautious referendum question, and proceeded with the referendum on May 20, 1980.

The P.Q. ran a relatively low-key campaign and promised that a "Yes" vote did not signal separation but only a desire to move in that direction. A later referendum would be called before any action was taken. In the interim, there would just be negotiations. The leader of the "No" side was provincial Liberal leader, Claude Ryan, albeit his actual position on Quebec's constitutional demands was ambivalent. Indeed, the P.Q.'s position was hampered in that many of its demands being raised had already been met. As Joe Clark had said during the campaign, "The Canada the P.Q. wants to secede from, no longer exists."

The decisive role in the campaign was played by Prime Minister Trudeau, who pledged that a "No" vote would not be a vote for the status quo, but would inspire the creation of a new constitution with a Charter of Rights and Freedoms guaranteeing the freedom and equality of all Canadians before the law.

The "Yes" side was defeated decisively in the referendum, obtaining only about 40 percent of the vote. Assuming all non-francophone Quebeckers voted "no," a majority of francophones rejected separation.

13.1.2 The Constitution

Buoyed by victory in the referendum, the federal government set about to reach agreement on a new constitution. Since the collapse of the Victoria Charter in 1970, whatever discussions were held on the constitution had been listless and generally unproductive. A typical attitude was expressed by one premier when he said that on the list of a 100 problems he faced, the constitution would rank 101.

In the months prior to his defeat in 1979, Pierre Trudeau had been unsuccessful in his constitutional reform efforts (even after making some wide-ranging concessions to the provinces). Now with a fresh majority government and victory in the referendum, Trudeau again called the premiers together and insisted that, if agreement could not be reached, he would unilaterally patriate the constitution—going over the Premiers' heads to enact a Charter of Rights.

Not all the provinces opposed the federal government. Ontario and New Brunswick supported Trudeau. The other English provinces along with Quebec opposed Trudeau's plans. Beginning with a Supreme Court challenge, the other eight provinces—soon to be dubbed, The Gang of Eight—established a common constitutional front.

Unsurprisingly, there was heavy opposition in Parliament both to the government's course and to the content of its constitutional package. As the proposal went through the long process of approval, even the British Parliament was involved. Finally, it was passed, highly amended.

The Supreme Court's ruling was inconclusive, albeit it did force one final federal/provincial constitutional conference. Here the federal government, by making one or two concessions to the provinces on the Charter of Rights, was able to split the "gang of eight" and win a compromise agreement which excluded Quebec. Thus the *Constitution Act of 1982* finally replaced the *British North America Act of 1867*. A *Charter of Rights and Freedoms* was also established, moving Canada somewhat away from the British system towards the American one. While both the constitution and Charter apply fully to Quebec, Quebec has never agreed to either. The essence of constitutional discussions since 1982 has been to develop an amending formula to which Quebec and all other provinces could agree. This issue has not been agreed.

13.1.3 The National Energy Policy

The new Liberal government was also prepared to act unilaterally on resources and energy. As the price of oil rose during the late 1970s, federal/provincial disagreements created the impression that the federal government was insensitive to western Canada's needs and without a coherent energy policy. It was, in a sense, the worst of both worlds. In 1980, the federal government announced *The National Energy Policy* (NEP). The policy was based on the belief that oil prices would continue to rise, and was an attempt to ensure a larger share of profits for the federal government. It was also an attempt to secure increased Canadian ownership and control of the industry, mainly through the expansion of the crown owned Petro-Canada. The plan also envisioned a vast expansion in oil exploration off-shore and in the high Arctic.

The Alberta government led the opposition to the NEP by threatening to reduce oil production. However, the crucial opposition came from the United States, which saw the NEP both as socialist and discriminatory. Brian Mulroney, soon to be Leader of the Opposition, compared the NEP to an early morning hold-up of a gasoline station. All of this would not have fazed the government—and public opinion generally supported the initiative—but the timing was bad. Oil prices began to slump, and the Canadian oil companies the program was supposed to support went bankrupt. American companies pulled their oil rigs out of Canada.

In 1981, Canada entered its worst recession since the 1930s. The Toronto stock market recorded losses of more than $20 billion. Interest rates rose to 23 percent, and in 1982, Dome Petroleum, the pride of the NEP, was saved from bankruptcy by a $1 billion government bailout. By that time, the Liberal government had been replaced by one pledged to dismantle the NEP, and the NEP was basically dead.

13.1.4 Canada/United States Relations

Canada and the United States had been in almost constant trade negotiations since the fall-out from President Nixon's economic policies in 1971. Various proposals for trade liberalization and sectoral agreements such as the Auto Pact always floundered over the issue of access to resources. The NEP had evoked outrage from American oil companies, and the American government had taken strong exception to many of its provisions which discriminated against American firms. But of greater concern to the United States, the NEP raised the issue of secure access to a vital resource.

Trudeau also infuriated the American administration by his continued friendship with Cuba and Fidel Castro, and his general downplaying of Cold War conflicts. In his final term in office, Trudeau struck out towards an independent foreign policy by demanding greater industrial-country support for third world economies. The Canadian government called for greater "North-South dialogue." Trudeau also engaged in a round of quixotic personal diplomacy, venturing to world capitals to propose measures enhancing East-West detente. His efforts bemused and bewildered President Ronald Reagan.

13.1.5 The "Walk in The Snow"

As he was to describe it, Pierre Trudeau took a long walk in the snow and decided to resign. Nobody was really surprised, nor sorry to see him leave office. Nationalism was apparently on the wane in Quebec; the economic situation had deteriorated; and Canada was looking for investment from any source. The Liberal Party was extremely weak—the 1980 election masked the fact that the party barely existed beyond Ontario. Canada wanted a change of leadership in style and substance.

13.2 Brian Mulroney

Brian Mulroney had been an activist in the Progressive Conservative Party from his student days. But as his career as a lawyer and businessman developed, he eschewed political office and contented himself with fund-raising and backroom strategizing. This changed in 1976, when he contested the leadership and was defeated by Joe Clark. After Clark's federal election defeat in 1980, his leadership was challenged directly and indirectly from several quarters in the party. While Mulroney's role in this period is murky, several of his supporters and friends played leading roles in the movement to dump Joe Clark. Clark was finally forced to put his leadership to the test, and at a leadership convention in June 1983, Brian Mulroney defeated him and became leader of the Progressive Conservative Party.

13.3 John Turner

John Turner was always considered a political rival to Pierre Trudeau. He had contested the leadership campaign against Trudeau and had served as Minister of Finance in the first Trudeau administration, but had resigned. Turner had returned to private practice as a lawyer, but maintained his political connections and played the role of heir apparent. However, when Trudeau resigned in 1979, Turner decided not to run for leadership. By taking himself out of the race then, most observers considered that he had retired from politics. With Trudeau's second retirement, Turner moved rapidly to claim the leadership.

13.4 The Federal Election of 1984

Brian Mulroney began campaigning from the moment he became leader of his party. First, he had to win a seat in the House. An obliging member with a safe seat in Nova Scotia resigned, and Mulroney won the by-election. But the real challenge for Mulroney, a Quebec native, was to win a seat in the Liberal stronghold of Quebec.

Mulroney set to work building a base in Quebec. In this respect, he continued with the work that Joe Clark and Robert Stanfield had done before—trying to end the party's isolation. Mulroney also courted the West, particularly Alberta. While Mulroney was campaigning tirelessly, the Liberals engaged in a huge round of patronage appointments. Turner was in one sense a helpless pawn in this process. Yet, as soon as he was elected leader, he called a snap election. It was a mistake; the only party caught off guard and unprepared was his own.

On September 4, 1984, the Conservatives won the largest landslide victory in federal parliamentary history, winning 211 seats compared to 40 Liberal and 30 NDP seats.

13.4.1 The Conservative Agenda

Margaret Thatcher was solidly in power in Great Britain and Ronald Reagan was moving toward his second term in Washington. Brian Mulroney and his revitalized Conservatives were kindred spirits, adapting the neo-conservative agenda to Canadian reality. In domestic affairs, this meant government retrenchment, privatization, and tax increases to deal with the massive deficits and debt built up during the recession. Mulroney had also to deliver on his promise to amend the constitution to reconcile Quebec within Canada. In trade and foreign affairs, Mulroney quickly aligned himself with the Republican administration in Washington. Within weeks of becoming Prime Minister, Mulroney spoke in New York to a select audience of business executives and announced the end of the NEP, and the recasting of the role of the Foreign Investment Review Agency from that of scrutinizing foreign investment to one of promoting investment. "Canada," he said "was again open for business."

As a candidate for leadership of the Conservative Party, Brian Mulroney opposed the concept of free trade. In office, and familiarizing himself with the state of Canadian American trade negotiations, he quickly reversed his position. The Canadian government shortly asked the American government to begin formal negotiations towards a free trade agreement.

These negotiations began amid a growing and highly emotional public debate. They became the major initiative of the Conservative government's first term. The *The U.S. Canada Free Trade Agreement*, while scarcely mentioned during the 1984 election, became the centrepiece of the 1988 campaign.

13.4.2 Quebec and the Constitution

The humiliating outcome of the constitutional debates cost Rene Levesque dearly. Quebec was in worse a position vis-á-vis federal government power than before. When the constitution was signed into law, Quebec could do little but fly the provincial flag at half staff. This symbol gesture of rejection reflected deep frustration within Quebec society. Mulroney, as he was building his coalition in Quebec, promised to redress this. However, there was no point in attempting to reopen negotiations with the P.Q. still in power in the province, although the party had dropped separation from its official platform and now seemed amenable to a new compromise constitution. But the P.Q. was split and clearly in the final stages of its mandate. There would be time after Levesque had gone. Meanwhile, Robert Bourassa, Mulroney's old friend and mentor, had returned to political activity and was "waiting in the wings" to become the once and future Liberal Premier of Quebec.